How to Eat
THE ELEP
in the Room

Digesting the Unspoken Truth

Eat me!

Kieran Hearty

Kieran Hearty

How to Eat the Elephant in the Room
Digesting the Unspoken Truth

First published 2014 by IGIVEU Publishing
Copyright © Kieran Hearty 2014

IGIVEU Publishing
59 Alfredston Place, Wantage
Oxfordshire OX12 8DL, UK
Tel: +44 1235 769814
Email: kieran@igiveu.co.uk
Website: www.igiveu.co.uk

ISBN 978-0-9928706-0-7
Editor: Chantal Cornelius (Appletree Publications)
Proof-Reading: Amelia Osborn
Cover Design and Typesetting: Clockwork Design
Printed locally by: Artisan Print Solutions

TESTIMONIALS

"Kieran Hearty's extraordinary advice and unique approach make How to Eat the Elephant in the Room an invaluable tool. Don't let the accessible humor inherent in this book fool you – Hearty is offering very sage advice. Do away with stagnation in your workplace and plan and achieve huge goals!"

Marshall Goldsmith, Author of the *New York Times* and global bestseller *What Got You Here Won't Get You There.*

"The only book on truth, trust and communication that you will ever need."

David Taylor, Author of the *Naked Leader Series*

"Kieran has taken a lifetime's worth of business and leadership experience and woven it into a hugely entertaining read that is topical, practical, and relevant. His book is jam-packed with wisdom and thought leadership, but most of all, he speaks the truth. In revealing the fundamental blockers to business excellence, he has created a piece of work that will make a huge difference to people who read it."

Carole Gaskell, CEO Full Potential Group.
Author of *Transform your Life* and *The Pocket Life-Coach*

"Anecdotes and stories bring serious business challenges alive in this relevant, practical and realistic book. Kieran Hearty manages to deliver an original and fresh perspective in answering some uncomfortable truths. If you're serious about upping your game in the 21st century this book is spot on."

Dr. Lynda Shaw, Business Neuroscientist and author of *Beat the Bullies: Use Your Brain*

"Kieran Hearty's way of bringing 'Elephant Nuggets' to life in an innovative and exciting way will draw you in to his menu of food for thought. Kieran's stories and research along with his absolutely fabulous passion for having more women in boardrooms is inspiring and refreshing. His vision and determination is catching and charming. I highly recommend this read. You will never look at elephants and menus in the same way again! In one word 'Fabulous!'"

Nicci Roscoe, The Mind Makeover Artist and author of *Fabulous Impact*

"Eating an elephant does not sound like an easy thing to do ... and it isn't. Kieran however, helps his readers to carefully navigate the process and it gets better with every course... especially as we learn from his insights and experiences. What I like most of all is, that by the time the After Dinner Speech happens, you are still wide awake, energised and ready for more."

Annemie Ress, Founder of PurpleBeach

ACKNOWLEDGEMENTS

This is undoubtedly the hardest task that I have ever undertaken, so my first acknowledgement is to all of my fellow authors. It has felt at times like being on a really tough, but rewarding, two year training course on how to write a book. Now I can't wait for the next one!

When I decided to write 'How to Eat the Elephant in the Room', my ambition was to write an entertaining and creative book about a difficult subject, but one that was highly informative. I said at the time that I wanted to showcase the work of a 'thought leader who knew his stuff', but in hindsight, I think that it was something that I simply wanted to prove to myself. The ultimate judge about the content of this book will of course be you, the reader.

I am very grateful to David Taylor (The Naked Leader) who loved the title, and gave me such strong encouragement to write the book. I am also grateful to Penny Ferguson, Bill Daniels, Jack Zenger, Carole Gaskell and Robert Baker for giving up their time to discuss the Elephant in the room with me.

I will be eternally grateful to my editor, Chantal Cornelius, who has walked alongside me on every step of this journey. Hiring Chantal was one of my better decisions.

Finally, I am permanently and indelibly gratefully to my wife Alison, who has been rock-like in her steadfast support, and saint-like in her patience and encouragement.

DISCLAIMER

No Elephants were harmed in the writing of this book.

MENU

APPETISER

This book was inspired by a keynote speech of the same title that I delivered at a conference in the beautiful city of Stockholm in November 2011. In keeping with an occasional tendency towards humour and irreverence that you may notice as you read the book, I successfully included the titles of five ABBA songs in my presentation without anybody in the audience noticing.

Key Ingredient – Elephant

We will explore the topical metaphor that is 'the Elephant in the Room'. As we know, a metaphor is a figure of speech that uses an image, story, or something tangible to represent something that is less tangible. It is a concept, or perhaps the germ of an interesting idea that we want to get across in an effective and interesting way. In much of the leadership work that I do, I stress the importance of story-telling and the use of metaphors to get your messages across to your audience in a variety of powerful and energising ways. I emphasise the powerful impact that words and pictures, as well as stories and ideas, can have in making messages real for our audiences.

A Bit about your Menu

This gastronomic feast of goodness is served up in four tantalising courses, each of which is designed to provide you with some delicious food for thought. Like all good dinners, the final chapter is presented to you in the form of an After Dinner Speech, the topic of which is very close to my heart.

The First Course is Elephant Nuggets. The Elephant in the Room is a complex beast that does not evolve overnight. There are different types of Elephant, whose growth can be triggered and accelerated by many different ingredients. We will conduct a detailed investigation and I will make a start in sharing some thoughts from people that I admire and whose opinion about Elephants I value.

The Second Course is Half-Baked Elephant. Not only is the notion of the Elephant in the Room somewhat absurd, but the degree of idiocy in play is quite shocking when one reflects on the sheer disproportion between the intellect that co-exists with this stupidity inside large organisations. Some of my exhibits are deadly and some are, simply, quite insane.

The Main Course is Elephant and Chips. Most of my career was spent working in high-tech organisations, of which eighteen years were spent with the technology company Intel Corporation, the largest ever manufacturer of micro-processors. Many of my beliefs and opinions have been formed, or informed, by the 'chip' industry. I have had some fantastic experiences and some less pleasant ones, the latter usually when I attempted to eat the Elephant in the wrong way. So, in this course, I will offer you the benefit of those experiences. I hope that you will learn from my mistakes with Elephants, as well as my more successful dining strategies.

The Final Course is Elephant Turnover. We will reflect on the staggering opportunity cost of the Elephant in the Room, which is such because there is a great deal of empirical evidence connecting the impact of Elephants on the bottom line results for many businesses. I will continue to develop components of our dining strategy in the belief that if we can successfully formulate and apply them in order to successfully eat the Elephant, untold riches and rewards will lie in wait for all of us!

Like ABBA, I too have a dream. I dream that there will be more women in boardrooms. I dream that coaching will be seen as a basis for competitive advantage. I dream that managers and leaders in all organisations will find a way to let go and empower people to truly perform.

A Bit about your Chef

After graduating from the University of Kent at Canterbury with a degree in Accountancy, I spent thirty-three years working for just four companies (ICL, Wang Labs, Intel Corporation and Lloyds Banking Group), of which ten years were spent with Wang and eighteen years were spent working at Intel.

For most of that time, I managed people, badly at first, but over time developing a reputation for my passion for developing talent. I never thought that I would end up in HR, but I found the perfect match for my talents and passions when I moved into the Learning and Development world in 1998. Since then, I have become an accredited ICF Coach, Coach Supervisor and Coach Mentor. I am also certified as an NLP practitioner, along with the DISC and Myers-Briggs behavioural tools.

After years designing a range of training courses and workshops and personally training thousands of employees, managers and leaders around the world, I fulfilled a long-held dream to set up my own company, which is called igiveu. I will tell you a bit more about the company, and the meaning behind the name, later in this book.

Food for Thought

It was no surprise to my family and friends that this book should have some kind of dining theme. As with all of my work in Coaching, Leadership Development, Management or Team Development, the ball is in your court. Any suggestion that I make, or idea that I offer, or story that I tell, is provided respectfully and, I trust, in a way that interests and entertains you. It is your choice what you do with it.

How to Eat the Elephant in the Room

FIRST COURSE

Elephant NUGGETS

"To know the Elephant, is to eat the Elephant"

In this First Course, we explore the metaphor – the meaning of the term 'the Elephant in the Room'. It is an expression that is becoming very popular these days as we hear it mentioned more and more in the media. I have therefore prepared a selection of tasty morsels for you to enjoy with me as we conduct our voyage of culinary discovery and, eventually, figure out how to eat the Elephant.

In Chapter 1, Potted Elephant, I will share a few examples of the different types of Elephant that tend to be discussed most often. I will also introduce you to a few of the people that I admire and ask them to share their opinions about the Elephant and its origins.

In Chapter 2, the title is somewhat self-evident in its intent. E.L.E.P.H.A.N.T. S.A.N.D.W.I.C.H. is a pretty substantial acronym. It gives us the framework to explore and to get on the table the vast number of ingredients that, in a variety of ways and for a variety of reasons, contribute to the growth of our metaphorical Elephant. It is a smorgasbord that may give us some of our first grains of food for thought.

Once we have started to explore the metaphor, using a combination of tongue-in-cheek humour, outrage and depressing facts, we will start to lay out our range of ingredients. This will help us to appreciate more easily what has been going on in so many organisations for such a long time. Some of it will be obvious; some may be a surprise, or even a shock. You may disagree with what I say and that's OK because disagreement is healthy and an important requirement for eating Elephants!

The formation of the DNA of the Elephant is a thing of great complexity and can take a long time to arrive at its final state of maturity, or immaturity, depending on which way you look at it. In this battle to eat the Elephant, we must never, ever, underestimate our adversary. It is not only a battle of wits; it is a battle for our very survival. We all need to be careful what we eat on occasion, because the risk of chronic indigestion, or even death, is never far away where Elephants are concerned, so please digest carefully as you read on!

CHAPTER ONE

POTTED Elephant

Elephants are mammals – they are pre-historic creatures from far beyond the Neanderthal age. We can find a lot of old fossils that prove they have been around for a long time. Certain types of Elephant are now extinct.

Some are not...

Mark Twain wrote a story in 1882 called 'The Stolen White Elephant'. It was about the inept, far-ranging activities of detectives trying to find an Elephant that was there all the time. The Oxford English Dictionary gives the first recorded use of the phrase, as a simile, from The New York Times on June 20 1959: "Financing schools has become a problem about equal to having an Elephant in the living room. It's so big you just can't ignore it."

I cannot remember exactly the first time that I heard the term 'Elephant in the Room' but I am fairly sure that it was when I worked at Intel. I think it was said after a meeting where an HR Leader in the room was working hard to avoid giving straight answers to questions about work-life balance.

It may be stating the somewhat obvious to say that the term 'Elephant in the Room' is a metaphor, or another way of saying:

"An obvious truth that is being ignored or goes unaddressed."

Many years later, I reflected on subsequent references to the Elephant in the Room muttered by frustrated or bewildered colleagues, for a variety of reasons. Just recently and, as far as I am concerned, unsurprisingly, the term is growing in popularity. Here are a few examples.

An Inconvenient Truth

In 2006, a former US vice president opened his new film: "I am Al Gore; I used to be the next President of the United States." The name of the film was 'An Inconvenient Truth', which focused on his global efforts to educate the public about the severity of global warming and the climate crisis.

There are plenty of conspiracy theorists who believe that massive amounts of money, political influence and misinformation campaigns are being thrown at many governments, in order to manufacture controversy, undercut the scientific consensus on climate change and downplay global warming's projected effects. Despite the broad international scientific consensus, allegations have been made that researchers and institutions that have produced the conclusive data about global warming are themselves part of a global scientific conspiracy.

He who must not be named

As a Harry Potter fan, I am familiar with the frequently used term "He who must not be named", that was whispered fearfully by many of the book's characters, by way of reference to the evil Lord Voldemort. It was as if to merely mention Voldemort by name would lead them to a terrible fate – as sometimes it did! And so the evil myth grew and grew. Even when Voldemort was many miles away, he continued to instil fear across an entire society, even amongst his closest followers.

He who should be named

The CEO of a large company stands up in a large auditorium in front of all the employees and tells them how wonderful things are and how lucky he is to have such an amazing team behind him. His senior team, almost all male, stand behind him on the stage, nodding approvingly then applauding his inspirational words.

In the audience, things are somewhat different. Most of the employees are unhappy and exhausted, as well as being fed up that they have to constantly look over their shoulder to see who is next in line for punishment under the company's brutal performance management system. Engagement figures are low and continue to fall quarter after quarter, yet the senior team blame 'external factors', proclaiming that 'green shoots' are just around the corner.

The employees all believe that they have a dysfunctional leadership team who are out of touch with them and their customers and only care about themselves. They also believe that if they speak up, they will almost certainly be fired, just like their ex-colleagues who had the courage to do so and are now flourishing elsewhere. To them, their much-vaunted 360 degree feedback system is a joke. Nothing happens about the feedback and they are certain that there are HR people, under orders from above, carefully scrutinising the 'confidential' feedback in order to weed out dissenting voices.

Yet things were so different when the founder of the company first started in that garage in Silicon Valley twenty years earlier. That early buzz of excitement is now replaced by a sense of weariness and wariness. Now, there is pressure from analysts about quarterly results, there are bosses who lose their temper at small things and criticise subordinates in public, sudden resignations, anti-trust lawsuits, increasing customer complaints, profit margins sliding and people blaming each other rather than supporting each other.

Problem – What Problem?

How many of us bury our head in the sand rather than risk hearing bad news? Let me give you an example. Consider the 'war for talent'. You may have heard this expression being used over the past ten years and you may very well have dismissed it as hysteria.

I remember speaking at an event many years ago and sharing the stage with a speaker from the Institute of Employment Studies. He shared some research data about the way in which workforce demographics in the UK, Europe and USA would change dramatically as the Baby Boomers started to retire from 2010 onwards. A key part of the data was the shrinking workforce in the 25-40 age range, which as we know is a key source of future talent in most organisations. It is now 2014 as I write and the problem has arrived, except that it is currently being masked by tough economic conditions and a double-dip recession, which, I might add, is a direct result of not addressing many of the issues that I will be sharing with you in this book.

Because of the tough economic climate, I have described the war for talent as a phony war. But the war is looming and most of us are woefully unprepared for it. This is not like the Y2K Millennium Bug problem – it will be a real war, with winners and losers. The winners will be those who heed my words and start working on their people strategy now, with urgency, because you are already behind enlightened companies who already do this.

All you need to do is to look at the companies who regularly feature on the Sunday Times Top 100 – they are the companies with the kind of cultures that talented people will want to be part of. Yes, you might still be able to 'buy' top talent from the annual University milk-rounds, but the price is about to go up. Heed my words!

I read a recent report by the talent measurement company SHL entitled 'UK risks leadership time-bomb'. Their research shows that the UK has slipped from 3rd in the world to 21st for the future supply of potential leaders, with Mexico, Turkey and Egypt occupying the top three places.

Many years ago, when I used to teach TQ (Total Quality), I talked about the post-war industrial renaissance of Japan and how the USA lost huge market share to Japan between 1950 and 1980 in areas like steel, automobiles and electronics. The Japanese won by listening to an American – W Edwards Deming – and applying his teachings. The USA lost by ignoring Deming and by being arrogant and complacent. In typical fashion, they waited for the crisis to occur before they reacted, by which time it was far too late. Are we going to make the same mistakes with people? Or are we going to pay the penalty for the many mistakes that we have already made? Are we going to wait for the crisis to occur? Maybe it's already too late.

For me, the war for talent is an inconvenient truth and many companies will wait for the crisis to occur before they react. This will be a very expensive mistake.

But I digress. There I was talking about Harry Potter and suddenly I'm talking about TQ and workforce demographics.

I asked a number of good friends of mine for their opinions about the Elephant in the Room. I am keen to share the thoughts of these people that I greatly admire and not just because I don't have all of the answers.

One of these people is Penny Ferguson, who runs a company called The Living Leader, named after her book of the same title. I still chuckle when I think about how I met Penny. Her PA had sent a speculative personal letter to Intel's CEO, Craig Barrett, and it ended up on my desk. I was about to 'file' the letter when I caught sight of the words Personal Leadership and decided to read the letter, check Penny's website and arrange a meeting.

I have worked with Penny several times since that day and have found her to be one of the most authentic people that I know. She is far from perfect and has made many mistakes in her life, but lives and breathes the NLP belief that "there is no failure, only feedback". Her Personal Leadership Program has positively impacted over 40,000 delegates globally and draws from her own life experiences. Many female colleagues have been inspired by Penny. I remember one senior colleague who I invited to attend one of Penny's programs. He was not considered to be a great leader, but changed overnight, for the better, as a result of attending the program.

I asked Penny what the term 'Elephant in the Room' meant to her as a metaphor for leadership and what immediately came to mind for her as the main contributing factors.

Here's what she said:

"For me, it boils down to just one thing and that is lack of trust. You can give it different names, such as fear; and whilst fear is a big one, fear is still about lack of trust. The challenge for me with that, which we see again and again, is when people too often, even at the most senior levels of an organisation, say what they think the boss wants to hear.

Have the courage to say what you think, even if you are wrong, or you have a misplaced version of events. For me it comes down to that every time."

CHAPTER 1: Summary and Final Thoughts

The term Elephant in the Room is a metaphor. It is a highly symbolic figure of speech, or image, which conveys the idea of the 'unspoken truth' that exists in organisations. A very good example of this is in Al Gore's 2006 documentary film 'An Inconvenient Truth', where if you ignore or deny the facts about climate change, then global warming does not exist.

The same unspoken truth applies to many other areas in organisations, including how the leadership of the organisation is really viewed by the employees. I have heard too many complaints from different people who I have met over the years describing their culture as 'toxic' and their leadership as 'dysfunctional' for it not to be real in many organisations today.

Heed this warning if you ignore the facts about your own organisational climate, or the looming war for talent. You can deny the truth, intimidate others against speaking the truth, or try to sweep the truth under the carpet. Ultimately, that path leads to disaster, as proven so often by events that I will describe in later chapters.

Do not ignore one of the biggest challenges that you face in many organisations, and that is lack of trust. Once trust is gone, you have successfully planted the seeds for your demise. Build trust by encouraging all of your people to speak up and say what they really think and not what they think you want to hear.

How to Eat the Elephant in the Room

CHAPTER TWO

E.L.E.P.H.A.N.T. S.A.N.D.W.I.C.H.

Elephants are Vegetarians

This is the longest chapter in the book by far, because as I mentioned earlier, we have a vast amount of ingredients on our table to consume. Please digest each selection of ingredients with an open mind and savour the food for thought that they may provoke.

I do not expect you to agree with everything that I put on the table. In fact, I insist that you disagree, where you feel that you have an alternative perspective to offer. I love disagreement, because it provides the energy that drives great decisions, great teamwork and great outcomes.

You may also notice that many of the ingredients seem to be very attractive and potentially quite delicious. Well, yes, they are. My wife Alison keeps telling me to eat in moderation, something that I have always found to be very hard to do. As a result, my weight and my sense of well-being have fluctuated wildly.

Good things, if abused, will eventually be damaging.

E is for Effort, Expertise and Execution

Many years ago, when I worked at Intel, I overheard a conversation about a senior manager there, which ended as follows: "... but we can't afford to get rid of him, he is too talented."

On a different occasion, I was preparing a communication and asked the General Manager if there was one key message that he wanted to get across to his organisation. He replied: "I want them to give me every erg of energy they can find." His message was all about huge amounts of Effort. I was never certain how true this was, but the senior leader mentioned above had a reputation for not looking approvingly at any member of his organisation who had personal interests or hobbies, as they were an unnecessary diversion from work focus.

At various stages of my career, I recollect female colleagues, with young children, who had very little flexibility in their working hours. They were fabulous at their jobs and probably twice as productive as many of their, typically male, colleagues. However, their lack of commitment counted against them at performance review time, in favour of those colleagues who worked longer hours.

I once conducted a 360 degree survey of all the managers in my geographic region, including the senior leadership team. For the senior team, a shocking 12 out of the 13 management competencies scored mostly below average, while the only high scoring competency was Expertise. In other words, they knew how to do the work. Now, let me say this for the record – expertise is important. A lack of expertise may very well be a fatal flaw that affects your overall value to an organisation as a leader.

In Chapter 9, when I mention the work of Jack Zenger and Joe Folkman, based on their 'Extraordinary Leader' research, it will show that expertise, or 'Personal Capability' as they describe it, is one of the five key pillars of 'extraordinary' leadership. Their evidence shows that expertise only provides a fraction of the required leadership capabilities or pillars and, taken alone, will not make you a great leader. It's a bit like trying to eat a nice meal of Elephant nuggets on a dining table that has only one leg.

I would add that it's a different kind of expertise to a simple knowledge of how the work gets done that is required. When I share one of my models, about Career Chasms, in Chapter 7, I will also share some thoughts from one of my favourite authors, Ram Charan, who said that one of the five signs of a misplaced manager of managers is "a single minded focus on getting the work done".

A large company that I know well was deciding which external leadership developer to work with and liked the JDI Model of Potential, developed by consulting company YSC, which was derived from the ratings of 10,000 psychological profiles. The company decided to work with YSC, but on one condition, that they added an E to their JDI Model, where E is for Execution. I was discussing this at the time with the HR Director of PepsiCo, who also used the JDI Model of Potential with their leaders, and he said: "Why on earth did they do that?" I will not mention who the company was, but they are in Financial Services ...

We live in a world where a single minded focus on results is pretty much everything. It is the shortest and quickest way to personal reward. It is hard to be an effective leader who builds long-term, sustainable competitive advantage when many market analysts applaud the behaviours that generate short-term results, but with potentially catastrophic long-term effects. It says a lot that many market analysts, also in Financial Services, place huge financial bets based upon such myopic short-term thinking.

L is for Leadership, Listening and Lingo

I once read a white paper by global consultants CCL (Center for Creative Leadership) in which they talked about a leadership development program that they developed in partnership with Barclaycard. Barclaycard commented: "We needed a leadership strategy that was connected to the larger vision and business strategy." When I read this, I couldn't help feeling a bit cynical, as I thought about Bob Diamond, who had just been forced to resign as Barclays' CEO, as a direct result of the LIBOR fixing scandal. (L is also for LIBOR by the way, which I'm saving for Chapter 4.)

I retrieved my copy of the 'Wall Street' DVD, just so I could hear the famous Gordon Gecko "Greed is Good" quote one more time. In my view, greed is at the heart of so much that is wrong in organisations today, (sadly, there is no G in Elephant SANDWICH), and I will explore greed as part of a larger exploration of Self-Serving Leadership. Obviously, Leadership is at the heart of the metaphor and, let's face it, there are good leaders and bad leaders. But so many business leaders make it ridiculously easy for us to point the finger at them in this respect.

However, in order to truly understand how to eat the Elephant in the Room, it is of fundamental importance that we first seek to understand its evolution, in a forensic, almost Darwinian way – hence the detailed exploration in this chapter of the large number of ingredients that have contributed in some way to the evolution of the Elephant.

For example, leaders did not arrive at their lofty positions fully skilled-up in the art of poor Listening. No, they acquired this lack of a critical leadership skill at an early age and refined it rigorously, closing their ears to so much valuable input, information and suggestion. Think about all the great decisions that they could have made, if only they had been open to the possibility that subordinates had better ideas, or worse, better information, than they did.

In my detailed case study in Chapter 3 about NASA, I will submit that poor listening and even poorer leadership were directly responsible for the loss of seven lives in the 1986 Challenger Shuttle disaster. I will also mention the BP Deep Water Horizon oil spill, where the same issues not only cost needless lives, but also caused huge environmental damage.

For those leaders who believe that the art of great communication is one-way, there is bad news. You are part of the problem that is undoubtedly affecting your reputation as a leader and probably the results that are achieved by your organisation.

Great salespeople, for example, know that great listening closes more deals. It is unwise to presuppose that the one-way part of a leader's communication style is the most effective one. During the Final Course, I will spend some time exploring how great leaders communicate and will give that context using a simple, non-time-consuming leadership approach called GIVE.

It is notable that the further up many organisations you go, the weirder and more unintelligible the language, or Lingo, becomes. The use of acronyms, jargon, buzz-words, abbreviations, long words and sentences that mean nothing becomes ingrained, creating the epidemic of 'corporate speak'. This leads to the side-effect of management speak that ignores big negative issues and attempts to spin them as positives. Here are some examples of corporate speak:

"This year we have seen significant negative growth."

"I just need to communicate that out to you."

"We're worried about bad cosmetics being aired publicly." (Enron Memo)

"We have to poke holes in this new idea or it could bubble up and become a show-stopper."

"We need a firm-wide focus on our throughput, even if that means redundancies in our clients' bills."

"Must be able to think in the sky, and dig in the dirt." (Twinings Limited job advert)

It's amusing, but I do wonder what's going on inside the heads of people in senior positions who feel compelled to utter such garbage? (I would never do it!)

E is for EQ, Ego, Efficiency and Email

Many of us have copies of various books by Daniel Goleman about Emotional Intelligence. For years, he has been a kind of hero to me and as you read this book, you will be able to see for yourself the inspiration that he has provided me with as I apply many of his principles to my own thinking about the Elephant in the Room. I frequently refer to Goleman's six leadership styles in my leadership development work, the most damaging of which (Commanding and Pace-Setting) I refer to early in Chapter 7.

About ten years ago, I remember feeling baffled as well as weirdly amused when I heard him being described by a person who had met him as 'an interesting character'. I am very pleased to confirm that I have now met Daniel Goleman and he is a very interesting character indeed. He is a great guy, with a high degree of self-awareness, a compassion for people and a deep appreciation of the needs of others.

In October 2013, I was lucky enough to spend two days with Dan and his wife Tara in a 'Mind Whispering' workshop in Oxford.

Like Dan and Tara, I am deeply convinced that being aware of your own feelings and those of others is an important personal and leadership attribute. Then, being able and of course willing to regulate these feelings in yourself and others is just as important, using emotions, as well as behaviours and language that are appropriate to the situation.

We talk a lot about IQ (Intellectual Quotient). I happen to have a reasonably high IQ. It's not spectacular, but it gets me into the top 1% and is probably a factor in my love for intellectual challenges like Killer Sudoku, Chess, Bridge and The Telegraph Crossword (easier than The Times).

High IQ is scarce and highly valued. Many of the big Financial Services companies in the city jostle for attention, armed with incentives, large starting salaries and guarantees of a rapid rise up the organisation, to lure the next batches of first class honours students from Oxford and Cambridge.

My IQ stays about the same, but my EQ improved as I became more self-aware and started to practice what I preach. EQ (Emotional Quotient) is an alternate descriptor of Emotional Intelligence and in the remainder of this book, I intend to explore it in a variety of ways.

I have mused, thought, even obsessed, about how to enhance EQ levels across organisations and have a few ideas, some of them my own, that I am keen to share with you. EQ is very important, not only on the leadership side, but on the personal side as well.

Far too often, we wait for the damage to be manifest before we try to fix it (or not).

Let's not forget that the people who eventually rise to the top, mostly started at the bottom. It was from those beginnings that they accumulated the skills, attitudes and knowledge (or lack of them) that defined their eventual path to leadership and the resultant culture that emanated from it. Think about this as you reflect on who you are as a leader, or a person, right now and then reflect further as you read the evidence that I present to you about the Elephant in the Room.

E is also for Ego. As we explore our dining strategy we will consider in depth the 'effective' leadership qualities that are essential for generating long-term sustainable results. For now, Ego is one of the ingredients that truly gets in the way of and strongly connects with so many other ingredients of the Elephant SANDWICH.

There is something that happens to many people as they climb the career ladder and acquire more status and power. They are consumed by an increasing sense of self-importance, and followers reinforce this by pandering to them, providing them with lots of positive noises, praise and good news. They start to believe their own press as the bad stuff is swept under the carpet. Eventually, they become more and more out of touch with reality.

Those of us familiar with Maslow's pyramid of needs will appreciate that we all have some healthy level of ego that needs to be satisfied. An over-abundance of ego can eventually lead to destructive outcomes, as the ego drives pursuit of power and fuels a self-promoting, self-serving culture, that will eventually have a corrosive and corrupting effect on engagement, reputation and business results. In Chapter 7, Elephant in Fiery Hot Red Sauce, there is an opening section called 'Red is for Danger'. There is more about ego there.

I want to briefly mention Efficiency and Email, two very interesting bedfellows in our list of ingredients. You may be surprised to hear that Efficiency is a quality that is associated with some of the behavioural traits that also sustain Ego.

Some people believe that efficiency is getting a lot done in a short period of time. In many ways, that kind of efficiency is an illusion, provided by fast-paced task-obsessives who like to keep lots of balls in the air at one time, but who leave a trail of mess behind for others to clear up.

In my opinion, the ideas that some people have about their own efficiency are at best misplaced and frequently myths. The inability of the 'too busy' leader to do the really important stuff is palpable. Their inability to formulate strategy, create plans, or even articulate clear goals and objectives makes a mockery of their single minded focus on effort and getting a lot of work done. Frequently, those who believe they are contributing and who expect to get rewarded for those prodigious efforts actually create long-term damage.

So, does efficiency seem like a good thing? Of course, but in the wrong hands, it can be an illusion. Email is a good thing, but how many emails do we receive and send every day and how many of these emails we send are a complete waste of our scarce time? I will contend that email, on its own, has a negative productivity impact of 20% on most organisations, which is not very efficient.

Unnecessary email, and the disrespectful behaviour that is poor email etiquette, glues us to our PCs and laptops when we could be doing real work and making a real difference for our organisations. I sometimes think that email is a problem of pathological proportions! And I haven't even got round to talking about Meetings yet – it's lucky there's no M in Elephant SANDWICH!

P is for Pay, Presenteeism and Power

We pay or reward people for their contribution to their employers. We have not yet completed the job of conning our people on the idea of 'discretionary engagement' to the extent that they will work completely for free, although exploitation of interns seems to be on the rise. It almost feels that there's a sense of entitlement by many employers to expect large swathes of free overtime from their people.

It rankles with me that some companies do a really fantastic job of making people so afraid for their jobs that they will regularly work 60 hours a week without a word of gratitude for doing so, let alone a penny in extra reward.

For many people, the pursuit of pay is a mission-critical thing. There are mortgages to pay, holidays to book and people to impress. Pay is one of the trappings of power, especially in Financial Services.

I do admire a strong work ethic, but like all good things, it can become not such a good thing if over-used, or abused. I will look at Workaholism under W, but Presenteeism is a curious thing. In essence, presenteeism is the opposite of absenteeism. The Wikipedia definition is "The act of attending work whilst sick", with this addition: "The tendency to stay at work beyond the time needed for effective performance on the job." Wikipedia continues: "... one could go to work due to a love and devotion to the job. In this case, presenteeism could be considered an act of organizational citizenship and inspire admiration from colleagues." It is a shame that such a heroic act makes other people sick as well and affects overall productivity as a result.

The Centre for Mental Health calculated that the cost of presenteeism from mental ill health alone (ignoring other contributory factors) is £15.1 billion per annum for the UK economy, while absenteeism costs £8.4 billion. Research shows that presenteeism is extremely expensive to employers, but all too often ignored: it is an unspoken truth. A survey by the Work Foundation reported that more than 40% of employees felt under pressure from managers and co-workers to come to work when ill.

Presenteeism, like so many other ingredients in our Elephant SANDWICH, is a direct result of our abject failure to focus on people to the same degree as we focus on results in the workplace. But here's the bombshell – we will accomplish far better results if we pay more attention to people and treat them in the right way.

Where do we start on Power? Well, you may know the old saying "Power corrupts, but absolute power corrupts absolutely". In the right hands and shared out in the right proportions, power is great. None of us minds a little bit of power now and then. It can be pretty motivating. In fact, while we are talking about motivation, I think of Frederick Herzberg, who was one of the first to research and explore what motivates and demotivates us at work. Herzberg's research showed that the top five motivators at work were: Achievement; Recognition; The Work itself; Responsibility and Advancement. The top demotivators included things like Bureaucracy, Relationship with one's boss and Pay.

David McClelland conducted much research into motivation and developed his Acquired Needs theory. This proposed that our specific needs are acquired over time and are shaped by our life experiences. Most of these needs can be classified under Achievement, Affiliation, or Power. On power, McClelland concluded that our needs lie in two areas – personal power (I want to direct others) or institutional power (I want to organise the efforts of others to further the goals of the organisation). Managers and leaders with a high need for institutional power tend to be more effective that those with a high need for personal power.

I am going to talk about Power Pie towards the end of this book (Chapter 9) when we will look at empowerment and powerful ways to achieve sustainable success by taking a slightly different perspective on power. For the moment, let me just put this thought on the dining table for you to chew over. The single minded pursuit of power is manifested in different ways and is connected to several key ingredients of our Elephant SANDWICH such as Ego, Hotshots, Advancement, Agendas, Self-promotion and Career.

Power frequently comes with baggage, especially as far as our reputation is concerned. For me, that makes power one of the key sources of oxygen for the Elephant in the Room.

H is for Hot-Shots, Hype and Habits

Do you remember the 1986 film 'Top Gun' starring Tom Cruise? When I think about Hot-Shots, I cannot help thinking about the famous line from Top Gun: "I feel the need, the need for speed!"

As a student of human behaviour and a practitioner in behavioural tools such as DISC and Myers-Briggs, I know that there are certain fast-paced behavioural styles that represent a preference for risk-taking and a certain need for speed. It is a perfectly normal behavioural style for such people, (I should know, I am one of them!), but this behavioural style comes with a health warning. I am going to spend a lot of time exploring human behaviour during the Main Course of this book, because this is fundamental to the rise of the Elephant in the Room and therefore a critical component of our dining strategy.

As I think about Hot-Shots in an organisational context, the term 'Key Players' comes to mind. These are the 'exceptionally able' people who have been identified as part of the future 'leadership pipeline' for their company. I remember one particular Hot-

Shot who had been identified for fast-tracking. He was delighted of course and broadcasted the news so that as many people as possible knew he was a Key Player. Sadly, at least three different co-workers swore that they would resign if this meant that they would end up reporting to him.

As ego continues to consume our Hot-Shots on their rapid rise up the career ladder, they are also consumed by a sense of their own self-importance. They puff themselves up and start to believe their own extravagant press, or Hype. They make powerful grunting noises designed to impress their cooing followers and instil fear in their competitors. Their use of corporate speak becomes increasingly widespread and proficient. Their CV and LinkedIn profile are riddled with it.

Hype is short for Hyperbole, meaning exaggerated statements. Very interestingly, it is also short for Hyperactive (an abnormal level of activity), Hypercritical (of others, but not self) and Hypersensitive (to feedback or perceived criticism from subordinates) which can create high levels of Hypertension in organisations – not very healthy.

Habits are practices that are very hard to give up – like continuing to do the same things we were rewarded for before we were promoted to manager. The definition of insanity is doing the same thing over and over again, expecting a different outcome. How come then that we fail to provide those managers who continue working harder and harder on personally getting the work done themselves with the urgent psychological treatment that they so badly need?

This is an issue of such Elephantine proportions that I will devote much time and culinary energy to it when we explore The Two Chasms of Leadership in the second half of Chapter 7.

A is for Alpha, Aggressive and Afraid

I once read a Harvard Business Review article by Gill Corkindale with a great title: 'Alpha Females: Deadlier than the Male?' It was a good article, but I felt it somewhat glossed over the brilliant topic. The Alpha Females that I have seen in action tended to be trying to imitate their male counterparts and not doing a great job for the reputation of women in leadership as a result.

For some reason, reading the article reminded me of my keynote at a Talent conference in Dublin the previous year, where I first met the team from Catalyst, a non-profit organisation that expands opportunities for women in business. I had made my presentation earlier and was participating in a panel discussion when the important subject of women in leadership was raised by the audience. After sharing some nuggets of empirical evidence which supported my personal belief that women, if given the opportunity, are slightly better at leadership than men, I was strongly challenged by the other male on the panel. He violently disagreed with my hypothesis because most of the senior women that he had ever worked for were real bitches!

He was so passionate in this belief that his interjection came over as quite aggressive. That not only made me wonder what was going on for him, as he heard me talk in such positive tones about female leadership, but what was going on for the women that he had described as bitches. It was a horrible word to use, but I could appreciate where he was coming from, if indeed his experiences had been as he described. They had conjured up such strong negative emotions for him.

Why do so many people in senior positions, male or female, feel the need to be so Aggressive at work? (This is usually channelled downwards of course.)

Yes, men are from Mars and women are from Venus; and yes, there are hormonal and physiological differences. But in terms of normal, healthy, predictable human behaviour, we are largely the same, except that women have the slight edge when it comes to leadership, which makes it criminal that more women are not on boards.

On the whole, aggression and other demonstrations of negative emotions such as anger are driven by fear. I remember a woman in a senior level position, who was both feared and hated by many of her subordinates. She once admitted to me that as she walked through the car park to work each day, she was a quivering wreck. As Penny Ferguson said, being Afraid is a manifestation, ultimately, of a lack of trust. It is hard to accurately place a negative value on the extent to which fear is damaging the potential of organisations, but it is without doubt measured in many billions.

In the next chapter, I will share some examples which will not make comfortable reading. You need to read them, because if you are contributing to fear in your organisation, you are part of the problem. And we both want you to be part of the solution.

N is for Numbers, Noise, Nuisance and No!

I have fond memories of my time with Wang. After all, I met my wife Alison there and we are still married after 27 years! Those were the days, between 1980 and 1990, when Wang's Office Information Systems and VS Computer Systems rapidly gained in popularity. I have many anecdotes and opinions about the ten year rollercoaster that I experienced, from a small company enjoying the buzz of explosive early growth, to a large company that was on the verge of bankruptcy just ten years later when I left Wang and joined Intel. But for now, I want to talk about Numbers.

The oft-repeated mantra that I most remember at Wang was, "Do the Numbers!" It was the regular call to action for the sales force – in fact, for everybody – in the early days, when political incorrectness was de rigueur and telling a few white lies to get a deal was the mark of a great salesperson. Quarter by quarter and year by year, I could see what was going to happen as "Do the Numbers" took a grip on the very fabric and culture of the organisation and decisions were made that no sane leader would make today (or would they?).

I often tell the story about the truck that went round and round the M25 at year-end and I will tell it to you before the end of this book. When I do, I think you will understand even more the point I am making about how a single minded focus on results can ultimately lead to failure.

What do I mean by Noise? Well, if I think back to my days with Wang, I was making a lot of noise about some pretty insane deals that were being done in pursuit of short-term results. A lot of noise was being made right back at me, usually telling me to shut up and sign off the salesman's bonus.

As I look back, I feel mixed emotions. I feel some sadness tinged with a combination of incredulity at the strokes we pulled. At the same time, I feel a lot of affection as I think about the great times I had and the friends that I made and the future wife I met. I am going to deal with 'noise' in a particular way and it is critical that you pay attention when I do so!

When I run workshops on strategy, I talk about 'noise' as a key sign of 'strategic dissonance' – in other words, where evidence is emerging that there is a potential problem with the company's business strategy. The leader who pays serious attention to such 'noise' is more likely to win than fail. I have many stories at Intel, some of them in the public domain, where the noise was loud and the resultant 'strategic dissonance', made manifest by the loud noises being made by middle managers, was deliberately ignored, at significant cost and loss of market share.

As I look back at my time with Intel, going back to when Andy Grove was CEO, I realise that he, in his teachings, and Intel were as a rule, very open and very honest about mistakes that had been made. Andy referred to such noise as evidence of an impending 'strategic inflection point'. Intel was usually pretty swift about responding to mistakes. The bugbear for me was that they just left it too late to admit to the mistakes for my liking. Maybe it was a symptom of stubbornness, or perhaps arrogance, a trait that was levelled at Intel all too often. Or maybe it was just down to poor listening.

I will of course conduct any such reflections in a loving, supportive manner, but will maintain those reflections in keeping with the Intel principle of Constructive Confrontation! So, how well do Intel leaders really listen and respond to noise?

N is also for Nuisance and I do wonder how many Intel leaders had the leadership nous to create a climate where noise was encouraged and listened to, because of the difference that would make, rather than send out irritable noise-reduction signals. How many such nuisances got a performance message about their upward communication style at their annual review?

I remember a colleague at Wang whose nickname was "No Way!" Before I reflect further on the most used negative word in the business dictionary, I want to reflect on the difference between the word 'No!' and the word 'No'. I feel that I must do this because of the number of times I found it necessary to coach team members who struggled to say "No".

Many of the words that I am sharing with you that form the ingredients of our Elephant SANDWICH can, in the right hands and used wisely, be good things. Let's look at the word No! The addition of an exclamation mark implies the addition of a level of emotion to the word. This is significant and changes the meaning and intent of the word. Later, when we share our first bite of the Elephant in Chapter 5, I will explain why the words are less important than the message that is conveyed through tone, nuance and body language.

When considering the word No, I think about the importance to me of the word 'disagreement', when it comes to developing high performing teams. I also think about something that I refer to as 'deficit-thinking'. This is killing organisations today.

By the time I am finished with you on just these two areas, you could well be on the way to gustatory success in developing and refining the level of understanding required to build your dining strategy.

T is for Time, Task and Trust

This entire book is based on real experiences and real truths. Here is one of them. I was running a workshop for a group of senior leaders and decided to impress them with some nuggets of recent empirical evidence that proved the phenomenal business impact of certain leadership behaviours and practices. They got really excited by this. We talked about sustainable results and business outcomes, with a general agreement that this made great sense to a group like them who were strongly results-focused. It always amazes me when I ask a group like this to quantify the strength of their results focus – in this case it was exactly 200%.

The tone of the room changed as good intentions took hold and we had a very productive session, with many of the directors signing up as owners for the different leadership actions that were agreed. It was also agreed that the owners would report back on progress against their committed actions at a follow-up session two months later.

Here is my question. What do you think was the single excuse given for their failure to complete the committed actions two months later? Remember, these were actions that were driven by the guarantee of better results as a key outcome if the actions were completed. They were 'too busy'. There was not enough Time! Now, as you reflect on this, think how often this excuse is used by leaders in your organisation. The reflection for me typically was what on earth were they 'too busy' doing?

T is also for Temper and I experienced some of that when I pressed them on why they had not prioritised these actions. And thus I retreated once again, having finally learned that you do not successfully eat the Elephant by confronting it.

But what was going on here? A group, dedicated to results, who were 'too busy', who claimed not to have enough time to prioritise the very actions that guaranteed better results than those they were currently achieving?

So what were they really driven by? It's a fairly logical conclusion that they were not driven by results. How could they be? Because surely anybody that is truly results-driven will not look a gift horse in the mouth! Or will they?

It's all down to what gets rewarded (hence E is for Effort.) This is why single minded Task focus gets a lot of attention from me throughout this book. There are certain behaviours that are frequently recognised and rewarded in most organisations and single minded task focus is one of them. It is a behaviour that can become pathological and one which successful individual contributors will carry with them into management and leadership roles (of which Fred 'The Shred' Goodwin was an extreme example as CEO of Royal Bank of Scotland). Why worry about the big strategic picture when there is so much detail to keep you infinitely busy as a leader?

Let me share with you a frequently used phrase that I heard during the performance management process at Intel. The phrase was 'Sand Shovelled'. Now, whilst I am not a technologist, I do know from my 18 years at Intel that the silicon that forms the key ingredient for Intel products is made from high quality sand. I therefore understand the importance of sand for Intel. Thinking back, I'm wondering about the relative value of using such a term as a means of discerning relative overall contribution, so that a judgement could be made about who out-performed who in a 'ranking group'.

What are we to infer from such a comment? Well, let's not single out Intel, but look at any senior team, who ultimately set the tone for overall performance within their organisation. If they are too busy to perform the leadership tasks that enable their teams to outwit and out-perform the competition, thus guaranteeing better long-term results, what is it that they are really committed to?

The answer probably lies with a number of the key ingredients in this chapter, including effort and pay (bonus). But what catches the eye in the short term is driven by their overarching need to outwit and out-perform each other. And they achieve that by being seen to have shovelled more sand than their competitors on the leadership team.

As I write, the Intel CEO Paul Otellini has stepped down to be replaced by Brian Krzanich, who is rated very highly by some of my friends at Intel. I remember a story that Paul told many years ago about performance management, stemming from the days when Craig Barrett was CEO. During Paul's annual performance review with Craig, he outlined the many great successes that his organisation had achieved during the year, to which Craig replied: "Yes, but what did YOU do?"

As the leadership team, and therefore the rest of their organisation, are focusing on outwitting and out-performing each other through the effort expended in moving large quantities of 'sand' from one place to another and then presumably ticking another box on their checklist of sand shovelled, I wonder what happens to Trust?

Trust, as we heard earlier from Penny Ferguson, is, in her opinion, the single most critical factor in the growth of the Elephant in the Room. Leaders have so much to gain from building trust. They have so much more to lose if they fail to do so. There is an old saying:

"Trust arrives on foot – it departs in a Ferrari."

I tell a story about an ex-colleague that I admire. His name is Benny Ginman. I reminded Benny of a key moment at a crisis meeting in Helsinki, when he suddenly realised why a significant amount of business had been lost.

During the meeting, I asked "Where is trust in all of this?" Benny thought for a moment, and then exclaimed, "That's it!" He walked over to the flip chart and wrote:

"Trust is in the Tank"

This is corporate speak implying that levels of trust between customer and supplier were less than good. For me, this was an Elephant moment. The unspoken truth was now in the room and we were able to have a serious discussion about how to regain trust.

(It didn't get us anywhere that day because it was a big Elephant in the Room issue, but we could now focus on the real underlying issues that had eroded trust between the two companies.)

S is for Stamina, Stress, Silos and Self-Service

You need a lot of stamina to be able to shovel a lot of sand. Stamina, as a pre-requisite for potential, is probably one of the reasons that so many Financial Services companies recruit ex-Olympic athletes, or use training companies run by ex-Olympians. It's also probably why alpha leaders enjoy tough and challenging outdoor team-building events so much. You know, the ones that require a small team to carry a huge heavy log for 100 miles through swamps, up steep mountains and across rivers, having built a raft using flotsam, rusty oil-drums and bits of rotting twine, without food, while being bullied by ex-SAS facilitators, after which the weaker team members suffer extreme humiliation and contemplate suicide, thus cleansing the talent pool. Just like being at work on Canary Wharf!

S is also for survival and you need huge reserves of stamina to be able to survive the corporate grind these days, let alone outwit and out-perform your colleagues in pursuit of the next rung of the corporate ladder. I am smiling as I recollect a discussion with Benny Ginman about email, when he joked that he received so much email that he even took his laptop to the bathroom with him, as he could clear at least ten emails while he was there.

Stress is for the weak. We don't do stress in our organisation. A good friend of mine, Rod Ireland, joined Intel as an HR Manager in 1999, the year after I found my own vocation in Learning and Development. Rod is one of the best HR people that I have ever met and, in my opinion, he was instrumental in reducing long-term absence at Intel in the UK. He certainly inspired me to contribute towards his mission and secured a large slice of my budget.

In conversations with Rod, I felt it necessary to develop a code, so we described stress as "The S-Word". For me, this was another unspoken truth – a company that prided itself on being hard-driving and defect-intolerant, being unwilling to use the S-Word just in case a Pandora's Box was opened and too many people would suddenly feel that it was OK to suffer from stress.

Our strategy was to reduce long-term absence both by building resilience levels in individual employees and developing the emotional awareness and confidence in managers to recognise and eliminate the root causes of stress at an early stage before they became a problem.

I approached a good friend, Philip Underwood, for help. I told him that I wanted him to design and deliver a program called 'Building Resilience'. No title would have worked better for a hard-driving organisation. There is something very powerful and stamina-inducing about building resilience which 'fixes' those who cannot take the heat and helps them to cope more effectively with high expectations and compete more effectively against each other.

When I think of resilience in a certain way, I think of silos – those deep concrete bunkers that contain weapons of mass destruction, poised to be launched at you if you step out of line. The best form of defence is attack and people in silos are ready to get their retaliation in first. They trust nobody, except their own.

People who work in Silos are described as having a 'silo mentality'. A typical definition is: People in certain groups who do not want to share information or knowledge with other people or groups in the same organisation.

I think that there is a lot more going on than that. Think about where most of their energy is focused as they diligently perform their day to day tasks and think back to my thoughts on sand-shovelling. If their efforts were truly focused on outwitting and out-performing their company's external competitors, rather than each other, what might happen? They would not only collaborate and think more inter-dependently, they would willingly and voluntarily share ideas, information, knowledge and even resources in pursuit of that objective. But let's face it – they don't.

One physical symptom of the silo mentality is finger pointing. If something went wrong, it was some other department's fault, not ours. Sales blames Marketing. Marketing blames Engineering. Everybody blames Finance. And as for HR, where were they when we needed them? It's pretty selfish, but pretty typical and certainly one of the things so many people in organisations complain about.

I remember the results of one survey, where two of the questions were: "How well do you collaborate with other teams?" and; "How well do other teams collaborate with you?

"The results of the survey were broken down by group and showed conclusively that each separate group felt that they collaborated with other teams, but that none of the other teams collaborated with them. I am not easily baffled, but there you are.

Self-Service is not what you think it is (at least, not in this book!). I can't help thinking about the restaurants with the 'all you can eat salad bar', where some customers ingeniously manage to construct a 12-inch salad tower in a small bowl. Now, if it was down to me, I would put some rules in place which prevented these excessive self-servers from transferring the salad to another, larger receptacle such as a doggie bag, and not allow them to leave the restaurant until they had eaten all of the salad. But I digress.

As a disciple of the great Ken Blanchard (Author of 'The One Minute Manager' and 'Lead with LUV') I have been lucky enough to have been permitted to teach his Situational Leadership program for many years. I have also heard Ken speak passionately about leadership. Ken is on a personal crusade against self-serving leadership and I have seen him speak with great eloquence and humour on the subject and also with contempt for those who demonstrate this trait.

Many of the ingredients that I have already covered, along with a few others that we will be internally digesting later in this chapter, form part of the DNA of the self-serving leader, the person who puts himself or herself ahead of the needs of customers, suppliers, shareholders, or other employees in their organisation.

The good of the company is an afterthought, or of no consequence at all, to such a person. They may or may not have some of the sales, marketing or strategic skills required to outwit and out-perform the competition, but I can say with 100% certainty that they are super-skilled and experienced in competing effectively with colleagues who stand in their way. They will do whatever it takes to achieve their personal career objectives, regardless of casualties.

When I think of the self-serving leader, I think of a great white shark that is prowling through the oceans in constant, merciless, cold-blooded pursuit of its next meal. Who do you know in your organisation that fits the bill?

A is for Ageism, Agendas and Autocratic

I remember when I decided to leave Intel. I was not ready to set out on my own, as I did three years later, so I decided to find another job. Even though I was successful, I considered myself lucky to have done so, and so quickly, because I was well over 40! I remember feeling relieved that I didn't have to state my age on CVs or job applications. I also remember a couple of jobs that I didn't get after a couple of interviews because I was 'over-qualified' and I remember decoding that feedback into a single word – Ageism.

I remember with great shame, when I worked at Wang many years ago as a Manager in my late twenties, reading through a pile of applications for a junior position in my team, rejecting one application from somebody who was in their 50s who said in their application, "... and I still have some good years in me". I could not imagine such a person fitting into my young, energetic, thrusting team, in such a fast-moving company as Wang was at the time. I hasten to add that I atoned for this sin of ageism on many occasions later in my career and made many successful hires of excellent people with great wisdom and years of experience.

How many times have we huddled around the coffee machine and talked about other colleagues behind their backs? I would be lying to you if I said that I have never done such a heinous and disrespectful thing. Have you ever used or heard phrases like "He's got an agenda"? If my Agenda is all about me, then I need people like me in my team and they are going to be young and cool like me, not old and past it. For the self-serving leader, it's all about their personal agenda.

But we've covered that kind of agenda already in some of our other ingredients. What about the agenda that we have in meetings? Firstly, how many meetings have you attended that had no agenda, or a poor agenda, or an agenda that was never adhered to, where you left the meeting feeling frustrated and that your time had just been wasted?

Towards the end of this book, during the Final Course, I will return to meetings (and email and other Elephant stuff) where I will contend that ineffective meetings and meeting practices, on their own, have a negative productivity impact of at least 20% in most organisations. Surely this is all meaningful when we collaborate on building our dining strategy.

In Chapter 3, Killer Elephant (Served Rare), one of the things I am going to discuss is the terrible impact of Autocratic leadership. Most of us know the kind of behaviours that we are talking about here – the behaviours typified by frequent bursts of intolerance and anger, berating people in public and constantly telling the best people not only what to do, but how to do it. Add to this poor, almost non-existing listening skills, creating an environment of fear, where bad news is banned, looking with contempt at anybody who spouts touchy-feely rubbish. Directive, controlling and impatient, the autocratic leader is hard-working and has a single minded focus on results through unilateral decision making, possibly a workaholic and, who knows, possibly in therapy! For some, an unlikely autocratic leader was Steve Jobs. What was it about him that was so successful?

I remember catching sight of the title of an article once which said:

"Autocratic leadership works until it fails."

Does this mean that there is a presupposition of eventual failure by using this approach? In my opinion, one or two autocratic leaders may get lucky and achieve short-term success. There is a case for sparing use of a directive leadership style to suit the situation, in the short term. In the longer term, the only possible outcome is failure, or worse, catastrophic failure.

How many times have we heard people say "But how have they gotten away with it for so long?" Think back to the comment I shared earlier: "But we can't afford to get rid of him, he's too talented."

Two different types of fear drive each statement. For the first one, think about the 'Lord Voldemort' effect. If I speak ill of my leaders, or criticise them, or give them unfavourable feedback, even if under the guarantee of confidentiality, it is certain that I will be found out; and it is certain that I will be severely punished, probably fired.

For the second one, the key fear is of losing the leader's intellectual property, which is more important than their people skills, EQ, or leadership capability.

For both of these examples, you need look no further than Financial Services.

N is for Normal, Narrow, Nature and Neuroscience

Thankfully, there are not too many psychopaths or complete idiots in charge at the top in companies (although they do exceed the norm by about 300 %). Leading or ruling entire nations seem more attractive to some of them.

Normal, predictable behaviour lies at the heart of the Elephant in the Room. Much of my work focuses on the following premise: that a lot of the things that quite rightfully look like good things, at first, start to become a problem later because of overuse or lack of fitness for purpose when the high performer progresses into the role of manager or leader of people. In other words, a lot of the factors that contribute to the development and growth of the Elephant in the Room are driven by the oxygen of good intentions.

Few incompetent leaders deliberately set out to become that way. The problem for them is that their measure of success, very much like their measure of effective contribution, was driven by a single minded, linear, upward trajectory of movement, hopefully exponential, in the right direction, whether it was work-related or career-related.

It is that Narrow, single minded approach that blinds so many future leaders to what it really takes to succeed and sustains them on a track that will inevitably be destructive, not only to others, but to their very reputation, as they see the long-term impact. The definition of narrow-minded is 'Rigid or restricted in one's views, intolerant, prejudiced, biased, opinionated, one-sided, parochial, petty, rigid and unprogressive'. How can we change that paradigm into a more abundant, broad-minded approach? Perhaps it's not in our Nature.

I sometimes describe myself as a student of human nature and by this I don't mean sitting people-watching whilst drinking a large espresso on the terrace of the Café de Flore in Paris. As we approach our last few bites of Elephant SANDWICH I want to say again that this entire menu is all about normal, predictable human behaviour and our reaction to it, which is, in itself, normal and predictable. The problem is that we're too busy to take the time to understand, or even discuss, what it all means to us. Have you ever heard somebody say "It's in our nature" to describe, or even to justify, certain types of human behaviours?

Human nature is a wonderful, multi-faceted thing. Wouldn't it be wonderful if we could all learn a little bit more about human nature and this normal, predictable human behaviour stuff, especially if we know how massive a difference that new understanding could make for us in terms of future relationships and future successes?

I will introduce a piece of my own work on human behaviour called 'Quarkiness' in Chapter 5. Please keep an eye out for it. A new awareness may emerge for you that could become dangerously addictive!

I want to explore Neuroscience in a bit more detail because it is not only fascinating, but highly relevant to us as we reflect on the dining strategies that may have a bearing on successful Elephant consumption.

I attended a conference in 2011 which was all about the relationship between the Coaching profession, of which I am part, and Neuroscience. It gave me much food for thought as a coach, but even more as author of this book and I am keen to share it with you. To start I would like to introduce just one part of the brain, the pre-frontal cortex, which is also known as the 'executive function', or 'seat of judgement'.

The pre-frontal cortex is surprisingly thin at just 2-4mm and enables us to regulate our emotions and make good decisions. For me, the metaphor of a filter springs to mind. The pre-frontal cortex can only process 3-7 chunks of information at a time and its ability to process information, regulate emotions and make good decisions declines with fatigue.

What does this mean for those in senior leadership positions who work long hours, under constant pressure and complexity, probably with insufficient sleep? The sickness absence of Antonio Horta-Osario, the CEO of my last company, Lloyds Banking Group, due to extreme fatigue, is a case in point and I wonder to what extent it is the tip of the iceberg. It's certainly food for thought.

D is for Defective, Dysfunctional and Directive

D is also for disease, many forms of which infect the workplace. I have much to say about what I describe as a defect-intolerant mind-set, which is pervasive in organisations and destructive when applied to people as opposed to 'things'.

Connected with this Defective form of leadership thinking is something that I and others describe as deficit-thinking. I am going to mention two other things that are pervasive in our workplace and which are powerful examples of the deficit-thinking mentality. They are Total Quality and Performance Management.

Let me say from the outset, that in the right hands, these are both wonderful principles. The problem for me is that they are frequently in the wrong hands and that is where severe damage may be done.

In the wrong hands, those of the deficit-thinker, Total Quality is based on the presupposition that our systems, processes and the way we work are never good enough. We therefore continuously seek out defects in order to fix them and improve our performance. With Performance Management, in the hands of the deficit-thinker, our people are never good enough and we must put systems and processes in place that help us to efficiently weed out the shirkers and remove them, or at least punish them in some way as an incentive to improve and perhaps "Pour encourager les autres". (This comes from Voltaire at the time of the French Revolution. It is used nowadays to describe an act of punishment that is out of proportion to the act itself and which is designed to encourage the others to shut up and keep their heads down.)

My use of the word Dysfunctional is inspired by the work of Patrick Lencioni and relates to his book 'The Five Dysfunctions of a Team'. One of my greatest Elephant challenges was a senior team who gloried in the fact that they were dysfunctional. Looking back, this provided me with the rich battleground that enabled the valuable failures, along with the occasional successes, which have inspired my leadership philosophy in the past fifteen years.

I frequently talk about directive behaviour in many of the workshops that I teach. Directive is a highly relevant word at all levels of development. Think about how you feel when you are new to a job and know very little about the new tasks that you will be asked to perform. Your boss is friendly and supportive and shows great belief in you. After all it was them who took a chance and hired you, because they liked the cut of your jib and thought you had potential. They are happy to let you get on with things and figure out how to complete the tasks because they have every confidence that you will be a quick learner. The initial enthusiasm you had when you arrived for work on your first day soon disappears, replaced by frustration and other negative emotions, including anger that you are not getting the direction that you need so much. What do you think of that nice guy who gave you a chance now?

On the other hand, you have been in the same job for a few years and really know how to do your job inside out. You are extremely competent and new team members seek out your advice. You really enjoy your job. A new manager arrives and from the first day, tells you not only what to do, but how to do it. They keep looking over your shoulder, checking for mistakes. How do you feel when this continues? You have been meaning to tell your new manager that you need no direction, but somehow, you don't feel that they listen and you feel that they would not react favourably if you said anything. What will that eventually do to your performance?

We use the phrase 'micro-manager' a lot to describe managers and leaders who closely observe and control the work of subordinates to an excessive degree. When you lack the competence required to perform a task and receive some direction, it feels supportive. But when you constantly receive direction, even when it is not required, that can have a corrosive effect on your performance, not to mention your motivation and morale. If you are a micro-manager, you are the Elephant's friend.

W is for War, Women and Workaholism

In Chapter 1, I mentioned the war for talent and the phoney war that we are currently experiencing in most western economies. It is the kind of War zone where, unlike EQ, the principles of Quantitative Easing are in abundance as governments print more and more money to help us to recover from the effects of many Elephants in many rooms. The war-like attitudes of many of the alpha male leaders may contribute to acceptable cultures where greed is good, customers are described as 'muppets' and great leadership is in as low supply as the availability of loans for small businesses.

One book which adorns many a CEO's coffee table is 'The Art of War' by Sun Tzu. In the book, Sun Tzu says: "Anyone who excels in defeating his enemies triumphs before his enemy's threats become real." This is a statement that will resonate strongly with the self-serving leader who successfully outwits their internal competitors and in strategic planning meetings uses powerful, war-like words such as 'annihilate', 'attack', 'destroy' and phrases like 'use overwhelming force' against the competition to 'hit 'em where it hurts'.

The thing I find about the concept of war is that there are winners and losers – the victors and their spoils. I have no problem, in principle, in strongly but ethically competing with other companies and outwitting them in the marketplace to secure a greater share. It is when the extrinsic becomes intrinsic that we have a problem, in my view: seeking warriors to fuel your talent pool is more likely to harm your future long-term prospects than enhance them.

Take Women, for example. I intend to deal with the important topic of women in leadership in a lot more detail during the Final Course of this book. Just for a moment, let's return to the talent conference that I attended in Dublin, where my personal admiration for female leadership had been challenged.

During the conference, I met some very interesting people from Catalyst, including their President, Ilene Leng and their European Director, Eleanor (Tabi) Haller-Jorden. They invited me to their team meeting after the conference and shared the results that they had compiled from research about women in leadership. I want to share two nuggets from that research.

The first was that there had indeed been an improvement in the previous 20 years for women in the boardroom. It was just one per cent. One per cent in two decades!

The second nugget, and primary reason for this pitiful, shameful improvement, despite all of the diversity effort that had been thrown at the problem (because it is a problem) over those two decades, was stereotyping. Men really do feel that they are superior to women. Being completely frank with you, a huge question for me is to what extent do women agree with them?

This takes us nicely to Workaholism. W is for Wikipedia which says: "A workaholic is a person who is addicted to work. The term also implies that the person enjoys their work; it can also imply that they simply feel compelled to do it. There is no generally accepted medical definition of such a condition, although some forms of stress and obsessive-compulsive disorder can be work-related. Workaholism is not the same as working hard. Despite logging in an extraordinary amount of hours and sacrificing their health and loved ones for their jobs, workaholics are frequently ineffective employees."

How many organisations reward such people and promote them into more and more senior positions where they can render large numbers of people just as ineffective as themselves and then continue to reward and promote them for it? I once said, in a moment of frustration: "Even a headless chicken could catch the eye around here!"

I is for Immediate, Intellect and Inconvenient

A few years ago, I created a workshop entitled 'Leading at eSpeed in a Complex World'. The pressure for immediate results, both internally and externally, is unrelenting. We have become so uncompromising and impatient that, in our personal life, we may even get irritated when unnecessarily delayed by an old lady at a pedestrian crossing for an extra five seconds.

I watched Usain Bolt win another three gold medals at the fantastic London Olympics and wondered to what extent we expect normal human beings to be able to work at world record pace for extended periods of time. If you can run 100 metres in 9.63 seconds, why not run a marathon in just 1 hour, 7 minutes and 44 seconds? Yes, this is stupid but I do wonder to what extent we place insane expectations on people that can only have a limited number of outcomes – failure, exhaustion or death.

I copied the following words from the internet, but sadly lost the link, so cannot attribute them to the wise person who said them. They are:

"We all know that the nature of the world and business is changing dramatically. We are moving at e-speed into an unknown world of the future. And the rate of change is escalating. Competitive pressures demand that product cycle times are shorter, resulting in the need for faster decision making. Though technology and market innovation are occurring in increasingly shorter timeframes, human capacity to respond to this rate of change is not developing as fast."

"All of this creates unparalleled demands on the attention of a

leader. Research indicates that leaders are receiving on average 190 messages a day via phone, email, etc. This combined with the pressures mentioned above, raises the spectre of overwhelm from the seeming chaos that we are living in. Many respond using previously proven methods. (Trying to work more, harder, longer...) However this is a time of discontinuous change, where old methods no longer work. It is not enough for a leader to redivide the allotment of time distribution on the pie chart. Instead, a new type of attention is required."

Earlier I talked about the significant imbalance between IQ (Intellectual Quotient) and EQ (Emotional Quotient) that can lead to the wrong kind of leadership and which can provide sustenance for the Elephant in the Room. In one sense, it would be hypocritical of me to mock the single minded focus that so many companies have in securing the best levels of IQ for their organisations, because I truly believe that Intellectual Capital is critical to competitive advantage. I just happen to believe that this means ALL of our HUMAN Capital and not just the intellectual elite.

Intellect is a wonderful thing, but it's not the only thing. It just represents one of the key strengths that people have – a very important one, depending on the type of business that you are in. But it's a bit like putting all your eggs in one basket in building the future competitive advantage of your company, if you then use a Harvard MBA or First-class Honours degree from Oxford as the basis for building your future leadership pipeline.

I know a lot of smart people who are capable of the most magnificent acts of leadership stupidity. At Lloyds Banking Group, one term used for some of the well qualified but mildly dysfunctional Oxford/Cambridge honours graduates in very senior positions, but without much in the way of interpersonal skills or leadership capability, was 'cone-heads'. I just love that description!

There's one thing about most smart people – they can 'get it' more quickly than others if given the opportunity to do so. This means that concepts like 'strategy' will come easily to them and they will be able to see through complexity and ambiguity. Here's a thought though. One might assume that smart people are not so stupid that they would ignore the wealth of empirical evidence that supports a certain form of successful leadership that will lead to results beyond their wildest dreams.

One might also assume that they would develop the additional skills with a similar level of commitment that enabled them to harness their intellect to secure their academic credentials. One might finally assume that they would readily adopt and demonstrate the specific behaviours that are statistically proven to work. It baffles and angers me in equal measure that they do not. Why are such clever people ignoring the evidence that is staring them in the face?

When the King of England, Henry II, said those fateful words about Thomas Becket in the extreme fit of temper for which he was both renowned and feared – "Will no one rid me of this troublesome priest?" – four of his knights took him literally and rode to Canterbury Cathedral where they murdered Thomas Becket on 29th December 1170.

Eight years earlier, against his better judgement, Thomas Becket accepted the powerful role of Archbishop of Canterbury from his good friend, Henry II, but prophetically warned Henry that their friendship would turn to hate. Their political differences had eventually become a great inconvenience.

To speak the Inconvenient truth sometimes requires great courage. I consider myself to be a bold truth-teller and encourage others to be the same, although experience tells me that there can be negative consequences of doing so! How can we create an environment where telling the truth is no longer inconvenient? How can we create an environment where vested interests do not try to sabotage the truth because it is inconvenient to their own self-serving objectives?

C is for Climate, Control, Career and Chasms

We mentioned the Inconvenient Truth above and this is a nice segue into Climate and Control. A phrase that I have heard a lot to describe a few leaders I have known was that they created 'a climate of fear'. For centuries, we know that this has been a tactic used by despots such as Vlad the Impaler, Adolf Hitler, Stalin, Saddam Hussein and many others; and we know the legacy that they left behind them.

I recently read an article about education in the UK which said that half of the UK's secondary school teachers were contemplating a different career. A survey of School and College leaders talked of "anger and frustration", with many complaining of 'bully-boy tactics' from the government and a 'climate of fear' brought on by both the Department for Education and Ofsted. Fred 'The Shred' Goodwin certainly created a climate of fear at Royal Bank of Scotland and look what that did to both his reputation and the future of one of the biggest banks in the world.

Of course when we think about the Elephant in the Room, what is the type of climate that they prefer? Is it a hot, demanding climate where sheer effort and sweat are the norm? A climate where it is all about survival of the fittest and "if you can't take the heat ..."?

The need for Control is real for some of us – for example, the directive micro-manager with borderline OCD tendencies. At its best, a healthy level of control provides us with good, sensible, positive boundaries within which people can be empowered to contribute and perform to their full potential. It provides us with a consistent set of rules and guidelines, designed to make life easier for us and not more difficult.

At its worst, control is a damaging thing which contradicts its original intent, which was to help and not hinder. There is good bureaucracy. This complements strengths and facilitates good work. Then there is bad bureaucracy which provides barriers to success and drives us towards failure. At the heart of bad bureaucracy lies an overwhelming desire to control people and things. This is not healthy.

Some people thrive on a Career which involves bureaucracy. Our career choices are driven by many things; sometimes it is just circumstances and other times it is by design.

For some, the word career has a sense of upward movement and we usually express this by drawing a straight line at an angle of 45 degrees, as if there is indeed an inevitable linear upward progression.

I remember criticising an HR Director who expressed his visceral reaction to HR colleagues who had a "strong sense of entitlement". I suggested that whilst I agreed with the words, I rejected the intent that he had used behind the words. Within the context that he had used, what about their entitlement to be treated with respect by their HR Directors and to be allowed some reasonable work-life balance?

Where I agree with the less positive view about a sense of entitlement is very much in line with my earlier comments about other ingredients such as effort, expertise and a few others. Many of us do take a fairly linear view of our career trajectory and have clear expectations of upward motion, but with scant idea of the different rules that apply at the different inflection points along the way. These are where the definition of insanity takes effect; and if you continue to assume that doing the same things will have a different outcome, you are in danger of falling into a very deep hole, or Chasm.

The other danger is that you may take others into that hole with you. This is not good for business. By its very nature, the word chasm implies a great divide between current state and desired state. (For more on chasms, please read Chapter 7.)

H is for Half-Baked, Hazardous and Health

H is for help! I hate my horrible, hard-headed, hateful boss who hassles and harangues me at every opportunity. It's only a matter of time before we haemorrhage people from this team because of his haphazard, Half-Baked approach to leadership. He is a hypocrite and his harsh, hostile, heinous, heavy-handed behaviours create havoc and make us all feel helpless. H is for Hell!

Now, where was I with his 360 degree feedback? Ah yes, I'd better put 'good' otherwise they'll know it was me and I'll be in trouble.

The definition of 'Half-Baked' includes key descriptions like ill-conceived, lacking good judgement, lacking common sense, poorly planned, foolish and stupid. You offer a senior team definitive empirical evidence which proves that new people strategies will deliver startling results for their organisation and after initial enthusiasm, they reject the opportunity because they are 'too busy'. Now that's what I call half-baked.

When leaders create a climate of fear that blocks the essential noise which warns us that something is seriously wrong, because people are too afraid to speak up, then danger lurks ahead.

When leaders create huge pressure on the organisation for delivery of short-term results, to such an extent that cutting corners and routinely ignoring key safety measures are tolerated, then danger lurks ahead.

When people are so exhausted that their pre-frontal cortex is not working at normal levels of efficiency and their decision-making capability is impaired, then once again, danger lurks ahead.

The Elephant in the Room can be Hazardous and can affect your Health. All the factors that lead us into the path of danger to our health are avoidable. But we're 'too busy'. We are 'too busy' to be strategic and properly look ahead in order to effectively plan our future and create a sense of purpose that guides us in the right direction.

We are 'too busy' to develop ourselves and our people, in order to equip them with the right skills that will make us more competitive. We are 'too busy' to listen to people who have the answers that we need to succeed, or be safe. The question that persists for me is what exactly it is that they are doing that is making them so busy, because they are working incredibly hard at not being a leader!

CHAPTER 2: Summary and Final Thoughts

A single minded focus on things that seem attractive and worthwhile at the outset may ultimately lead to an unhealthy outcome.

It could be the single minded Effort that leads to Workaholism, Presenteeism, Stress and Hazardous corner cutting. It could be a lack of Leadership, which is replaced instead by self-serving Ego and a single minded focus on Power, where bad Habits are embedded into the culture, creating Agendas, Noise and eroding Trust. People become Afraid to speak up, so the truth becomes unspoken and a short-term focus on the Numbers becomes the norm. Leaders are selected based upon their Task focus rather than their strategic capability.

Stress becomes an unspoken word, where it is all about the survival of the fittest. Those who are best suited to survive in such a culture are rewarded for their Autocratic leadership style, where a Narrow-minded approach flourishes, at the expense of not only individual reputation, but of that of the Dysfunctional senior team which values such behaviours. It is a team where Women are not welcome, unless they demonstrate the deadlier alpha female characteristics. Or maybe it is the single minded focus on superior Intellect coupled with an all-consuming Career focus that results in the Half-baked cone-heads ending up in charge of large organisations that are singularly lacking in Emotional Intelligence or any form of people skills!

All of this may be uncomfortable, but it helps us to get the unspoken truth onto the table, because to know the Elephant is to eat the Elephant...

SECOND COURSE

HALF-BAKED Elephant

Elephants have thick skin.

They can thrive in places where other mammals cannot.

Elephants can take the heat.

I mentioned at the end of Chapter 2 that the definition of 'Half-Baked' comprises elements like ill-conceived, lacking good judgement, lacking common sense, poorly planned, foolish and stupid.

In Chapter 3, Killer Elephant (Served Rare), I will remind you that Elephants can be dangerous, especially if you make them angry. They may try to frighten you by making loud noises and if that doesn't work, they may attack you. Sometimes, Elephants may kill you.

As we look at NASA, BP and the UK National Health Service, we will scrutinise the role of poor leadership and other factors and how they contributed to the injury and death of other human beings, all of which was one hundred per cent avoidable. Even more frighteningly, it was all predictable.

In Chapter 4, Sub-Prime Rib of Elephant, a large amount of focus is subtly implied in the chapter's title. After a career in high-tech, I was so obsessed by what was happening in Financial Services that I decided to investigate it first hand and spent three years there as an undercover investigative reporter for this book. OK, I'm exaggerating a little, but I had the opportunity to experience that type of culture for myself.

I will spend some time looking at the LIBOR scandal and the Barclays culture; I will offer some thoughts as to what has driven these pretty reprehensible cultures.

CHAPTER THREE

KILLER Elephant (Served Rare)

Elephants make a lot of noise when they are angry.

They may try to intimidate you.

If an Elephant stamps on you, it hurts!

On 25th May 1961, US President John F. Kennedy said: "I believe that this nation should commit itself to achieving the goal, before this decade is out, of landing a man on the Moon and returning him safely to the Earth." Now that's what I call a magnificent goal – a significant strategic decision, which excited many people, for many years.

On 28th January 1986, the Challenger Space Shuttle took off. In its crew of seven was Christa McAuliffe, the first female teacher in space. Just 73 seconds later, Challenger broke apart and plummeted into the sea. Although the exact timing of the death of the crew is unknown, several crew members are known to have survived the initial breakup of the spacecraft. However, the shuttle had no escape system and the impact of the crew compartment with the ocean surface was too violent to be survivable.

The Rogers Commission, appointed by US President Ronald Reagan to investigate the accident, found that NASA's organisational culture and decision-making processes had been key contributing factors. In this chapter, I am going to explore how poor leadership and a failure to listen needlessly cost seven lives.

On the evening of 20th April 2010, a gas release and subsequent explosion occurred on the Deepwater Horizon oil rig working on the Macondo exploration well for BP in the Gulf of Mexico. Eleven people died as a result of the accident and others were injured. The fire burned for 36 hours before the rig sank, with a resultant environmental disaster that affected millions of people. Poor leadership, a failure to listen and a gung-ho attitude to safety in the pursuit of short-term goals cost eleven lives and damaged our environment.

On 29th July 2010, I read the tragic story of four babies who died at the John Radcliffe hospital in Oxford. Managers were trying to raise the number of patients being treated in order to avoid closure and appointed a junior surgeon to carry out the extra work. Unfortunately, he was left alone on his second day. Despite raising his concerns about the ageing equipment, poor working practices in the unit and being unsupervised, his voice went unheard until he finally asked to stop working after four of his patients died within three months. The subsequent report cleared the surgeon of any wrongdoing, but criticised the lack of planning and support in the hospital.

Since that article was published, the NHS has been consumed by scandals about patient negligence and subsequent cover-ups. I have read the most shocking reports about poor leadership, bullying and negligent patient care, all of which have had a direct or indirect influence on hundreds of unnecessary deaths. I was shocked that an institution like the NHS could behave in such a way and as an ardent admirer of the nursing profession I found it hard to believe what I was hearing. What on earth had been going on?

KILLER Elephant

Case Study: Space Shuttle Challenger Disaster

Whilst I will try to be brief in the telling of this story, it is a very complicated one. You need to understand the complete picture of this lunacy in order to arrive at your own conclusions. I will offer my own at the end.

I first started using this as a case study in my leadership development work many years ago and have updated it for this book after digging deeper, looking for interesting articles and case studies. One case study that really inspired me was called 'Doomed from the Beginning' by Kurt Hoover and Wallace T. Fowler from the University of Texas at Austin and I have drawn significantly from it.

When the Space Shuttle Challenger blew up in January 1986, it was as a result of catastrophic failure of a key component of the solid rocket boosters (SRBs). The disaster was 100% avoidable and, in fact, had been predicted well in advance by many of the people associated with the program. They were intimately aware of the grand promises, funding shortfalls, cost-cutting and technical compromises, as well as the politics that had interfered with the Space Shuttle program from the outset. As a result, some of the key components were of inferior quality, including the O-rings that eventually failed at the low temperatures which had gravely concerned engineers.

There are three main contenders in this battle to be Elephants of the 20th Century. Firstly NASA, who made the decision to launch the Challenger Space Shuttle on that freezing cold morning of 28th January 1986; closely followed by Marshall Space Flight Centre; and Morton-Thiokol, based in Utah, who were responsible for manufacturing the solid booster rocket motors that were used to launch Challenger.

The sheer stupidity of some of the decision-making that I am going to describe to you (and the prevailing underlying attitudes and behaviours that drove those decisions) are quite breathtaking when you consider the level of IQ that permeated these organisations. But first, let's have a quick look at the history of the Shuttle program.

The strategy to build a space shuttle goes back to 1969, when it was approved by US President Richard Nixon. The final design, driven by cost considerations, comprised a reusable winged Orbiter, solid rocket boosters and an expendable external tank.

Marshall Space Flight Centre (MSFC) was, and still remains, NASA's designated developer and integrator of launch systems, with ultimate responsibility for the solid rocket boosters. When MSFC was formed in July 1960, it was led by Director Wernher von Braun, with Eberhard Rees as his Deputy Director for Research. They and almost all of their team came to the USA from Germany under 'Operation Paperclip' at the end of the Second World War. Whilst they were all excellent rocket scientists, most of them had been members of the Nazi regime and had made use of slave labour. It can be debated whether or not that had a bearing on the culture that later developed at MSFC. You have probably guessed my opinion.

We also know that William R. Lucas was named Marshall Director in 1974. During his leadership, Lucas was responsible for managing the Shuttle's propulsion system, including the SRBs and the main engines of the Orbiter. Lucas soon became known as a harsh taskmaster. He was a bully and frequently dressed down his subordinates in public, creating a system of dictatorial leadership, building a culture of fear in his organisation.

Lucas also had a reputation for dealing only in terms of hard, quantifiable data. This is questionable, because in the aftermath of the Challenger disaster, it emerged that key personnel at MSFC, including Lucas, were fully aware of the potentially catastrophic design flaws.

As we dig further into this story, we come to the decision to award the contract to design and manufacture the SRBs. Four companies had bid for the contract, of which the Aerojet bid was recommended by the NASA advisory panel. This was overruled in favour of the more expensive Morton-Thiokol bid by NASA administrator Dr. James Fletcher. Interestingly, Dr. Fletcher had been President of the University of Utah between 1964 and 1971 and had many political connections with the state and its industries. Whilst he denied that these connections had any influence on his decision, his vague rationale and inability to provide any solid reasons for the selection of Morton-Thiokol raised many unanswered questions about the ethicality of his decision, which Aerojet unsuccessfully appealed.

Utah is well over 3,000 miles from Florida, which meant that it was impossible to transport the SRBs as single units by rail, so they had to be shipped to Kennedy Space Center in sections, which were then bolted together. We will come back to this in a moment, but let's look at the configuration of the Space Shuttle as it would have been seen by onlookers as it prepared for launch.

The Orbiter (the fixed wing aircraft that glided to landing upon a successful return from its mission) was attached to a huge external tank, containing liquid oxygen and liquid hydrogen for the Orbiter's engines. The external tank was 154 feet long and just over 27 feet in diameter. Also attached to the tank were two thinner (12 foot diameter) SRBs of similar length which contained solid fuel, rather than the liquid fuel contained in the external tank. The SRBs were reusable and provided 80% of the overall thrust required at lift-off. After approximately two minutes, the SRBs would separate from the external tank and, using parachutes, descend slowly to the ocean below, where they were recovered. The external tank was not reused and would be jettisoned once low earth orbit was achieved. It would then burn up in the atmosphere.

Single unit rocket boosters containing liquid fuel would seem to have been the sensible choice, but it looks as if sensible choices were at a premium. Liquid fuel is preferable to solid fuel because it can be restarted and is easier to control. Once ignited, a solid rocket burns to completion and cannot be shut down if there is a problem. Engineers at MSFC were not in favour of solid fuel, but after much internal debate, the decision, driven by cost and political considerations, was made to use solid rockets despite their inherent dangers. Funding challenges and political pressure forced NASA to make many decisions purely on the basis of immediate costs, even if the longer term costs would be significantly greater as a result.

So Morton-Thiokol manufactured the SRBs in four casting segments, into which the solid fuel was poured, or cast. These four factory joints were shipped by rail to Kennedy Space Centre. Because they now contained solid fuel, the factory joints could not be welded together and were assembled by stacking, then bolted together.

The joints created by the assembly process were called 'field joints'. The sealing problem that led to Challenger's fatal destruction occurred in one of the field joints, when hot combustion gases from the SRB leaked through the joint and either weakened or burned a hole in the external tank, producing the catastrophic fireball that was witnessed by the world.

The well-documented root cause of the sealing problem was the O-rings, which are widely used in machine design; when they work properly they can seal enormous pressures. The sealing in the field joint was achieved using a primary O-ring, backed up by a secondary O-ring. They are made from a synthetic rubber material called 'Viton', which was further protected from degradation by the hot combustion gases by a protective layer of zinc chromate putty that was manually applied prior to assembly.

Key personnel at MSFC, including their dictatorial Director William R. Lucas, were aware of the potentially catastrophic design flaws. Many were not in favour of solid rocket fuel for manned spacecraft and had little experience in this area. In addition, the culture and management style did not encourage free discussion of such concerns or problems; when problems did develop with the SRBs, they were hushed up.

Despite these apparent attempts by MSFC to cover up the problems, they did leak out. For example, during the 1985 launch of Space Shuttle Discovery, the primary O-rings in both SRBs were found to be severely charred and, significantly, severe charring and degradation of a secondary O-ring was also discovered.

Warnings were issued by Morton-Thiokol engineers, based on major concerns about the effect of cold external ambient temperatures on the performance of the O-rings. The external temperature at the time of the Discovery launch in 1985 was 53 degrees Fahrenheit. Later in 1985, NASA Deputy Director Hans Mark issued a memo which recommended that the Space Shuttle should not be allowed to fly again until the SRB field joint problem had been adequately addressed. He resigned from NASA soon afterwards and the memo was never seen again.

On 28th January 1986, the overnight temperature was forecast at

23 degrees Fahrenheit, 30 degrees below the absolute minimum recommended ambient temperature for a safe launch, with the probable temperature at time of launch still below freezing. There are pictures of Challenger prior to launch which show significant amounts of ice.

Morton-Thiokol engineers, including Allan MacDonald and Roger Boisjoly, who later testified at the Rogers Commission, tried strenuously but unsuccessfully to delay the launch until ambient temperatures were at a safe level. I think it would be reasonable to infer a high level of certainty on their part that the outcome of the launch would be catastrophic. They all pointed to the Discovery data (at 53 degrees F) and all the engineers agreed that the colder weather would further decrease the elasticity of the O-rings. If this happened, the O-rings would seal more slowly, allowing hot combustion gases to surge through a field joint.

Allan MacDonald was Morton-Thiokol's senior representative at Kennedy Space Center. Part of his responsibility was to sign off the launch. He felt so strongly that Challenger should not launch that he refused to bow to huge pressure from both his employers and NASA.

There are a number of recorded conversations that took place with MSFC management just prior to the decision to launch. Morton-Thiokol engineers recommended a delay in launch until ambient temperatures increased to 53 degrees Fahrenheit, to which the aggressive MSFC management response was "prove that it is unsafe to launch!" (NB: This was a complete reversal of normal operating procedure as NASA procedure was to prove that something was 'safe'.) Faced with extreme pressure from MSFC, Morton-Thiokol management stepped in and over-ruled Allan MacDonald and their other engineers, giving NASA its approval to launch. 73 seconds after launch, the predicted catastrophe occurred.

Ronald Reagan immediately formed a Presidential Commission, The Rogers Commission, to investigate the Challenger disaster. Its findings were damning. One conclusion of the commission was that "Thiokol management reversed its position and recommended the launch at the urging of NASA and contrary to the views of its engineers in order to accommodate a major customer."

The Morton-Thiokol engineers testified that for years they had been discussing problems with the joints and their O-ring seals, especially in cold weather. The Rogers Commission concluded that managers at MSFC and Thiokol had known, or should have known, that the case joints were hazardous and thus had failed to prevent a predictable accident.

The Commission decided that since MSFC officials had prior knowledge of the hazard, the accident primarily resulted from ineffective communications and management. One fact missed by the Commission was that the Shuttle was never certified to operate in temperatures that low – there was no supporting test data to support any expectations of a successful launch.

The Commission also found that NASA's organisational culture and decision-making processes had been key contributing factors to the accident. Managers had known Morton-Thiokol's design of the SRBs contained a potentially catastrophic flaw in the O-rings since 1977, but failed to address it properly. They also disregarded warnings from engineers about the dangers of launching posed by the low temperatures that morning and had failed to adequately report these technical concerns to their superiors.

Allan MacDonald and Roger Boisjoly felt that had put their jobs on the line in order to try to prevent the catastrophe. They were not wrong to feel this way! After testifying to the Commission, both were removed from the investigation by their bosses. Both told the Commission that they felt they were being punished for their actions. In his book, 'Truth, Lies and O-rings', MacDonald wrote: "Roger and I already felt like lepers, but when we returned to Utah following the 2nd May session our colleagues treated us as if we had just been arrested for child sexual abuse."

MacDonald also wrote: "For some strange reason we found ourselves being challenged to prove quantitatively that it would definitely fail and we couldn't do that. I was probably more shocked by this dramatic change in philosophy than anyone else." It later emerged that NASA managers frequently evaded safety regulations in order to maintain the launch schedule.

Conclusion: The first article that I ever read about the Challenger disaster was in Harvard Business Review. I will never forget the comments by Richard Feynman, a brilliant mathematician and Nobel Prize-winning physicist who was on the Rogers Commission. There is a powerful YouTube clip of Feynman dipping a small O-ring into a glass of iced water to demonstrate the problem to his colleagues.

Feynman later said, in an article entitled 'Rocket science is not the hard part', that he had become so fascinated by the problem of fostering open communication in a large organisation that if he were starting over, he might study management instead of physics! As an eternal optimist, I always look for crumbs of hope in stories like this – key learnings born out of tragedy, that lead us to a different and brighter kind of future. I hope for a future where trust and open communications are the norm; where leaders listen to their engineers in order to make the right decisions for the right reasons and thus avert future catastrophes.

How naive we all are. On 1st February 2003, the seven crew members of Space Shuttle Columbia died when it disintegrated upon re-entry into the Earth's atmosphere. It was as a result of damage sustained when a piece of insulating foam fell off during launch and struck the left wing. In a chilling similarity to the Challenger disaster seventeen years earlier, engineers who were worried about the foam strike and who wanted pictures taken to assess the damage were stifled in Columbia's management meetings. I rest my case.

CHAPTER 3 – Summary and Final Thoughts

The evidence connecting poor leadership to avoidable impact on human life is overwhelming, yet apart from the odd political burnt offering, I see scant accountability.

I chose the Challenger Space Shuttle Disaster because it showed a pattern of unacceptable behaviour that evolved over time. Despite the absolute certainty of engineers that people would die, their grave concerns were not only ignored, but were shouted down by the evil Lord Voldemort and his henchmen at the top.

These sinister leaders put their own self-interest above people's lives. Adding insult to injury and death, they then sought to punish the people who had spoken up! Although this is just one case study, please consider the implications for many later scandals, where similar patterns of leadership behaviour were observed.

People do not always die, but the outcome of poor leadership is frequently and inevitably a disastrous one. I mentioned the BP Deepwater Horizon, where short-term goal focus drove managers to take short cuts with safety that led to problems which ultimately cost lives and an environmental disaster. I reflected on the sad case at a local hospital, also caused by a failure to listen. Sadly, this is just the tip of the iceberg for the NHS, where even their regulator suffers from poor leadership and I feel gloomy about the prospects for the future, unless radical steps are taken to deal with the overpaid, self-serving, bullying leadership that jeopardises the health and reputation of such a great institution.

CHAPTER FOUR

SUB-PRIME RIB OF Elephant

"I'm forever blowing bubbles, pretty bubbles in the air,
they fly so high, nearly reach the sky, then like my dreams
they fade and die ..."

Popular Cockney Song, 1919

This chapter is mostly about leadership in the Financial Services sector and I thought that it would be an easy chapter to write. I worked closely with Financial Services during my six years as a treasury manager with Intel; I have three years of recent experience as a senior manager in a major bank, with a wealth of ammunition at my disposal with which to craft a comprehensive, hard-hitting attack on the key source of recent woe for many millions of people and entire economies.

Far from being easy, deciding what to include in this chapter and what tone to take have been intensely difficult. This is mostly because of my desire to be as constructive as possible, in keeping with my mission to help you understand and eat the Elephant in the Room and not simply climb onto the finger-pointing bandwagon.

After all, who could forget Fred 'The Shred' Goodwin, chief

architect of the downfall of The Royal Bank of Scotland (RBS) or Bob Diamond, the aggressive chief of Barclays, who was forced to resign after the LIBOR scandal? Were you were affected by the Payment Protection Insurance (PPI) scandal? Have you have seen your hard-earned savings, investments, or pension funds negatively affected in the past few years?

I do intend though to allow a little self-indulgence as I explore what has gone wrong with banks and other Financial Services organisations and the role that inept leadership has played in this fall from grace. I will also allow myself a small taste of the self-gratification that was manifest in its abundance around those boardroom tables for many years.

I also intend to respect and to some extent protect the majority. By this I mean the good name of these once proud financial institutions and the vast majority of honest, ethical employees who work there, which has been sullied by the actions of a small minority of individuals, who abused their positions of so-called trust in a devastating way.

On 4th October 2008, after 18 years with Intel and a career spent entirely in high-tech, I joined Lloyds TSB as a senior manager responsible for leadership development. I was officially the last senior manager hired by Lloyds TSB before their acquisition of HBOS. My friends told me that I was mad. In hindsight, they were probably right!

Three years is not that long and certainly not long enough to have garnered a comprehensive insider view of Financial Services as a whole, but I have three things to say about Lloyds Banking Group. Firstly, they remain close to their roots as a solid utility bank and whilst not perfect, they are, in my opinion, the best out of what is mostly a bad lot in Financial Services. There are a lot of excellent leaders at Lloyds, but a fair few incompetent leaders as well, some of them 'cone-heads' and some of them prime examples of the intolerant self-serving leaders who are ruthlessly career-obsessed and who believe that they are exceptional.

Second, my opinion is that the HBOS acquisition in 2008 was a potentially great idea, driven in haste by self-serving ego and opportunism and then somewhat clumsily executed by a very small number of senior people, whose competence in my eyes was highly questionable. I fervently believe and hope that it will eventually succeed, albeit with avoidable opportunity costs and impact on people, which is my big issue.

Third and, disappointingly for me, a lot of the self-serving leadership that I witnessed was in the HR organisation. This is not untypical and not just in Financial Services. Maybe that is why I never felt that they really 'got' leadership.

Like others, I wondered to what extent having an American, Eric Daniels, at the top affected the overall culture. I also wondered if it was significant that the average age of leaders that I met on the HBOS side was substantially lower than on the Lloyds TSB side. These are just my own thoughts and, to be fair, I hasten to repeat that I worked with some excellent leaders from both the Lloyds TSB side and HBOS side. My final year with Lloyds Banking Group, as it then became, before I left to set up my own company, was rewarding. I was lucky enough to have a leader who demonstrated a unique blend of high intellect, expertise, results focus and people focus. I will not embarrass him by mentioning his name, but he has a fine operatic singing voice!

So, this chapter is an expression of my personal views about the impact that an aggressive form of self-serving leadership has had in creating the culture of greed that brought the banking system to its knees and in doing so has had such a far-reaching and long-term effect on entire economies.

We live in a world where many of our once dominant financial institutions are no longer credit-worthy. Indeed, as a result of the mismanagement and corrupt practices within Financial Services, entire economies, such as Greece, are being propped up by the EU. But this chapter is not about who is credit-worthy; it's about those who are not worthy of any credit whatsoever. So I would like to invite you to a new Awards Dinner, one for which I have created the perfect menu.

Enjoy ...

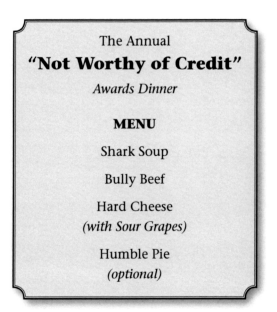

The Annual

"Not Worthy of Credit"

Awards Dinner

MENU

Shark Soup

Bully Beef

Hard Cheese
(with Sour Grapes)

Humble Pie
(optional)

Who I should invite to this Awards Dinner? There are so many unworthy candidates, but first, let me introduce you to our host for the event. It has to be the legendary rogue trader Nick Leeson, whose fraudulent, speculative trading caused the collapse of Barings Bank in 1995.

I'm sure that Nick will have many amusing anecdotes to share with us, including telling us about his time in Singapore's Changi Prison, where he wrote his autobiography, 'Rogue Trader'. Perhaps Nick can also speculate with us as to whether or not he feels Financial Services learned anything from his experiences.

So, without further ado, let's look at the different award categories.

The Annual
"Not Worthy of Credit"
Awards Dinner

PRESENTER: NICK LEESON

1. The 'Kermit the Frog Award' for Client Care

2. The 'Lord Voldemort Award' for World's Worst Banker

3. The 'Gordon Gecko Award' for role-modelling greed

4. The Lance Armstrong 'Omerta Award' for honesty

5. The 'Sub-Prime Sack of Shit Award' for integrity

The 'Kermit the Frog Award' for Client Care

Winner: Lloyd C. Blankfein (Goldman Sachs)

Lloyd C. Blankfein was nominated by Greg Smith, in his letter of resignation on 14 March 2012 from Goldman Sachs, where he says: "When the history books are written about Goldman Sachs, they may reflect that the current chief executive officer, Lloyd C. Blankfein and the president, Gary D. Cohn, lost hold of the firm's culture on their watch. I truly believe that this decline in the firm's moral fibre represents the single most serious threat to its long run survival."

The breath-taking arrogance of Goldman Sachs leaders continued into January 2013, with their highly publicised musings about whether or not to defer 2012 bonus payments until the new tax year, so that recipients could avoid paying part of their tax. They changed their mind after comments from Mervyn King, Governor of the Bank of England, who described their greed as depressing and accused bankers of misjudging the level of public anger at the damage caused by the financial crash.

So, congratulations to Lloyd C. Blankfein, who once described his role as a banker as "I'm doing God's work", and who created a culture where his leadership team felt comfortable about describing clients as 'muppets'.

The 'Lord Voldemort Award' for World's Worst Banker

Winner: Fred 'The Shred' Goodwin (RBS)

Fred got his nickname, not because of late night shredding of incriminating evidence, but as a result of his habit of sacking employees and ripping some of his most senior level subordinates to shreds, during his legendary daily 9:30am morning beatings.

Intimidation and humiliation were Fred Goodwin's tools of choice. One senior manager said: "Fred was never happy until he'd found somebody to belittle." Another said: "Fred had a very impressive intellect ... but he used that to bully those around him. People were intimidated from speaking their own mind because they feared Fred's reaction."

There are many leaders who are feted and richly rewarded for demonstrating the brutal alpha male Fred Goodwin leadership style. They truly believe that this delivers the best business results, defying all contrary empirical evidence about leadership. Look at the facts – in February 2009, with Fred Goodwin in charge, RBS reported a loss of £24.1B, the biggest in UK corporate history.

Congratulations, Fred, You are the World's Worst Banker.

The Gordon Gecko 'Greed is Good' Award

Winner: Bob Diamond (Barclays)

The new CEO of Barclays Bank, Antony Jenkins, recently told a parliamentary committee on banking standards that he was "shredding" the legacy left by his predecessor Bob Diamond. What Antony Jenkins was referring to was the aggressive and self-serving culture that had previously existed at Barclays, fuelled by their brash, American leader, Bob Diamond, king of the casino bankers, who brought that cavalier mentality into retail banking.

Barclays are not alone in having a 'greed is good' mentality, where the single minded pursuit of personal gain eventually supersedes integrity, people, or customer focus. Bob Diamond presided over the contribution of unscrupulous members of his organisation who conspired, with other banks, to fix the LIBOR interest rates over many years.

During his tenure, Diamond was described as "the unacceptable face of banking" and criticised for his level of pay and a lack of humility, which became manifest when he refused to stand down as CEO. Following widespread anger at his refusal to step down and amidst concerns that his presence could be harmful to the Barclays brand, he resigned on 3rd July 2012.

> ## The Lance Armstrong 'Omerta Award' for Honesty
>
> *Winner: Bernie Madoff (Investment Adviser)*

I wish that I could invite Bradley Wiggins to the Awards, to say a few words on behalf of Lance Armstrong, where he could share his experience about how it was possible for a British cyclist to win the Tour de France without cheating, without taking banned performance-enhancing drugs, or intimidating his team-mates!

Bradley Wiggins exquisitely summarised, in just three words, the thoughts of millions of people, when he said "The lying bastard" after watching Lance Armstrong's rehearsed performance during his interview with Oprah Winfrey.

In 2009, Bernie Madoff was jailed for 150 years for the biggest financial fraud in US history, in which his Ponzi scheme defrauded thousands of investors of about $18B.

The word 'Omerta' means a code of silence about the activities of a criminal organisation. In the case of Lance Armstrong, Omerta has been frequently and deservedly applied. A book called 'No One Would Listen' was written by Harry Markopolos about the frustrating efforts he made over a decade to alert the US Government, the Financial Services industry and the press about Madoff's fraud. It is easy to suspect Omerta but I suspect regulatory incompetence.

The 'Sub-Prime Sack of Shit Award' for Integrity

Winner: Warren Spector (Bear Stearns)

From 2005 to 2007, the investment bank Bear Stearns was one of Fortune magazine's most admired companies. Their casino banking bubble spectacularly burst in July 2007 after their disclosure that two sub-prime hedge funds had lost nearly all of their value amid a rapid decline in the market for sub-prime mortgages.

The risky Alt-A loans being issued by USA mortgage companies were processed into mortgage-backed bonds and other highly profitable investments by Bear Stearns, who became the number one underwriter of mortgage-backed securities.

Investors were deceived about the fundamentally defective character of the sub-prime mortgages underlying their investments and many of them sued the bank in 2007. In 2006 and 2007 alone, they incurred estimated losses of $22.5B on $87B of bonds sold to them.

Emails were disclosed which cited a Bear Stearns executive describing one investment as a "sack of shit". Bear Stearns was acquired by JP Morgan in 2008 and no longer exists as an entity. The above disclosures almost certainly triggered the financial crash that followed. Warren Spector, who managed both funds, was asked to resign as Co-President. He is now involved in film production.

Will we be forever blowing bubbles?

There is a wonderful article by the BBC's Robert Peston, entitled 'JP Morgan Sub-Prime Horror', which comments on practices which almost led to a banking melt-down in 2008. He talks about the "manic and frenzied culture of procuring and packaging as many mortgages as possible, to maintain the bonds spewing from the investment bank, to generate as much short-term profit as humanly possible."

There's nothing new here of course. Think back to the South Sea bubble, which burst spectacularly in 1720 after a UK-wide frenzy of investment by people from peasants to lords. Many people were ruined overnight and the Chancellor of the Exchequer, John Aislabie, was imprisoned not long afterwards.

Could it be that there is a frenzy of greed strand in our DNA code that automatically self-activates every fifteen to twenty years? Is it in our DNA that the smell of short-term profits switches on some kind of neuro-biological source code that causes us to behave in an aggressive, single minded and deceitful way?

Could this be the Elephant in the Room?

CHAPTER 4: Summary and Final Thoughts

There is nothing like a satisfying meal – and that Awards Dinner was nothing like a satisfying meal, apart from a few moments of self-gratifying irreverence! Meals like this leave us with the bilious feeling of acid in the stomach and a bad taste in the mouth, along with the nauseating reflux sensation of lessons not learned. The most indigestible piece for me is that despite the sheer size of many of these organisations, their downfall lies in the hands of a relatively small number of self-serving, egocentric, arrogant people. They were all in leadership positions and probably remain in denial, seething with indignation at their unfair treatment by the government, shareholders and the media.

I have a high regard for the good name of many of these financial institutions that have seen their reputations ruined and their long-term future jeopardised by such a small number of people. Many of them are not actually leaders. They have probably never been told the requirements of being a leader, nor were they rewarded or held accountable for being a leader. They have been richly rewarded nonetheless, which is the oxygen and vital nourishment that feeds the Elephant in the Room.

The results of any organisation are in perfect alignment with the prevailing leadership that is demonstrated within that organisation. If we reward the wrong behaviour, we leave the doors wide open for the most single minded and ruthless operators to succeed. It is easy to turn a blind eye when short-term results are the primary concern, but in the longer term, we reap what we sow.

MAIN COURSE

Elephant AND CHIPS

Q: How do you eat an Elephant?

A: One bite at a time.

Most of my career was spent working for just three technology companies, ten years of which was with Wang Labs, followed by eighteen years with Intel, who took the humble silicon chip and made it into something quite extraordinary.

I met my wife at Wang and made some close friends there. I experienced the excitement of explosive growth along with the anguish of disastrous decline. Moving to Intel, I once again rode the wave of rapid growth, made many friends, learned a great deal and witnessed a different form of decline, when the Intel stock price nose-dived in September 2000 and never really recovered.

It would be disingenuous of me to be anything other than open and honest about my experiences and in the expression of my opinions as far as Intel is concerned. I have a great deal of affection for Intel and in a desire to be transparent, approached a friend of mine in the Intel legal department, offering to disclose everything that I have written about the company. Intel may make great chips, but there are other areas where it has been less effective over the years and where it has been strongly criticised by many ex-employees.

In some respects, parts of this book feel like writing a letter to an old friend who, whilst successful, never quite achieved their full potential. One final point that I would make about Intel is that I would never compare the Intel culture to so many of the 'toxic' cultures that we hear about today. Intel is highly ethical as a company and lives and breathes uncompromising integrity.

In the remainder of this book, I will be sharing a lot of my ideas and my work with you. I have thought long and hard about how to express the next chapters to you and I would like you to start by memorising just four key words, each of which is at the heart of my message about how to eat the Elephant in the Room:

JUDGING

UNDERSTANDING

APPRECIATING

VALUING

In many different ways, these four words have inspired a lot of the work that I do as a Coach and developer of leaders and high-performing teams. If they are as helpful to you as they have been to me, then maybe, we can start to successfully eat the Elephant!

In Chapter 5, Silicon-Reared Elephant (with Quarks), I will explore the following question: What can we do to change the atmosphere in which the Elephant thrives? Introducing my first key word, Judging, I will lead you through a somewhat quirky voyage of discovery about the relationship between human behaviour at work and quantum physics.

In Chapter 6, Well-Grilled Elephant, my second key word, Understanding, leads us into the area of behavioural science, as well as exploring in depth the kind of things that happen to many of us who single-mindedly pursue a career upwards in the organisations that we work for and the damage that this does.

In Chapter 7, Elephant with Fiery Hot Sauce, my third key word, Appreciating, moves us into a different place. What if there is a different paradigm or atmosphere that is toxic for the Elephant in the Room, but is great for business and our reputation as leaders?

After some sweet waffling in Chapter 8, we come to our final key word, Valuing, in Chapter 9. It continues to amaze and humble me in equal measure that we all have the potential to easily make the life-changing move from negatively judging each other to positively valuing each other.

Now that we have a clearer idea of what our metaphorical Elephant looks like, the individual 'Bites' that I share with you in the remainder of this book are designed to give you some useful food for thought, as well as some powerful resources that will help you to eat the Elephant.

There is no best known method for eating Elephants and each 'Bite' that I share with you is merely an offering from me that I know from experience either works or will be helpful to you in the form of food for thought, not part of any meticulously planned systematic process. All I ask is that you keep an open mind as you digest each bite and then choose what will work for you, in what sequence of bites.

How to Eat the Elephant in the Room

CHAPTER FIVE

SILICON-REARED Elephant
(With Quarks)

"I have a memory like an Elephant.
In fact Elephants often consult me."

Noel Coward

Leader-hips – The Story of a Typo

I would like to start with the story of one of the most inspiring moments of my life. It was a moment that was inspired by a typing error and as I tell you this story, I will explain how it connects to my key messages in this chapter.

I was Master of Ceremonies (MC) at a conference in Budapest in November 2012. As a professional leadership speaker, I love being in the MC role, because it enables me to add value to the event in a number of ways. One way in which I do this for each presenter is by performing a function that I describe as 'topping and tailing'. I provide a cool introduction for the presenter and then, after they have completed their keynote speech, I summarise a few key points that I heard them make, which reinforces their message and demonstrates that I have been listening! I also provide continuity between presenters, ensuring that the event keeps to the timing on the agenda, and create a good vibe for the audience with one or two interesting or humorous comments of my own.

A few minutes before the start of the event, I was browsing through the conference brochure, looking for an interesting fact about the first presenter and there, in front of my eyes, was a glaring typing error.

At that moment, I had a choice. I could have reacted as so many of us would do in this instance and rolled my eyes in disapproval, muttering to myself that I knew these guys were second rate. Instead, I smiled and saw the potential that this typo provided me with and I immediately knew how I would introduce my first speaker. A moment later, I stood in front of the audience and said something like this:

"Ladies and gentlemen, I feel truly inspired and privileged to be able to introduce our first keynote speaker, because today, we have a world premiere. If you check your conference brochure, you will see that for the first time in history, we have a 'leader-hips expert' in the room!"

The audience laughed and 'leader-hips' became a theme for the day. I joked that it would become one of my keynote topics and that there would be a 'leader-hips' master class and even a book. It is now one of my regular speaking topics, there is a leader-hips master class and who knows, when I finish this book…

Judging

Let's go back to the choice that I made when I spotted the typing error. When I tell the leader-hips story, I reflect that most of us have a tendency to judge people who are different to us. It is a perfectly normal, predictable aspect of human behaviour, but this does not mean that it is a productive one.

We tend to judge other people and situations because we don't know any better. It's not our fault and in any case most of the time that we do this, our reaction is not overt, or violent, or abusive. Most of the time, our reaction is more likely to be covert, or even imperceptible. We might make a face, or roll our eyes, or mutter quietly to ourselves, or none of these things. But one thing is for certain – judging has occurred.

The reason that this is such a big issue for me is that judging happens all the time. It is a permanent fixture in the interactions between millions of people in millions of homes and offices across the world. It is a phenomenon that is universal. It transcends language, culture, gender and geography. We all do it!

This is such a big issue for me that I wanted to get it onto the (dining) table as soon as possible. Judging is responsible for behaviours that have the most corrosive effect on engagement, relationship potential and long-term business results. I told you that this would be an exploration of the relationship between human behaviour and quantum physics – that is why I have called it 'quarky behaviour'.

'Quarks' of Human Nature

A month after the conference in Budapest, in December 2012, I read that scientists at CERN in Switzerland had confirmed the discovery of the Higgs Boson. The Higgs Boson was predicted by the 'Standard Model' which describes the fundamental particles of matter and how they react.

The fundamental particles of matter that interest me (although for different reasons than the scientists at CERN) are called 'quarks'. They are elementary particles, smaller than protons and fundamental constituents of matter. There are six types of quark

– up, down, top, bottom, strange and charm. Quarks are sub-sub-atomic particles – they are very small!

My work, of course, covers a different part of the scientific spectrum. It is behavioural science, the study of normal, predictable human behaviour. In other words, it's all about human nature. It is work that's not conducted in an underground particle accelerator, but I am very open-minded and seek inspiration everywhere I can. So, inspired by quantum physics and the work of scientists at CERN, I too have developed a model, which I describe as 'The Standard Model of Quarkiness'.

The Standard Model of Quarkiness

I was giving a presentation at the London chapter of the Professional Speaking Association in July 2013, in which I introduced the term 'quarkiness'. The President at the time noticed this word on a flip-chart and pointed out my typing error!

Everything is connected in some way. It is a sobering thought that we humans, at a quantum level, are nothing more than clusters of vibrating sub-atomic particles interacting with each other.

As human beings, we spend most of our waking lives demonstrating quarky behaviour. When we notice something that we disapprove of, we emit strange quarks. When we notice something that we approve of, we emit charms. This may be a surprise to you, but in my standard model of quarkiness, it's very true. But what are they? How do we know them when we see them?

I described judging as a manifestation of our disapproval about people who are different to us. When we disapprove of something, we exhibit all kinds of small and sometimes almost imperceptible body language, facial expressions, noises and eye movements that reveal our true feelings.

We bombard each other with these tiny messages of disapproval, or strange quarks, which are picked up, if not always consciously, then by our finely tuned semi-subconscious antennae. In fact, once this quarkiness is revealed and understood for what it is, things will never be the same again – we notice all of it!

I was walking down the street one day with a good friend, who had her arm linked through mine. As we walked down the street the following conversation took place:

Her: "Did you see that?"

Me: "See what?"

Her: "Ooh…if looks could kill."

My friend is black and what she had referred to was the 'look' that we had received from a couple who had just passed the other way. I had noticed nothing, but then again, I am not black. She had picked up some microscopic body language, in this case an almost imperceptible facial expression, or quarky behaviour, that expressed disapproval at a black lady walking arm in arm with a white man.

If we had confronted the couple who had just passed us, they would have been distraught. As far as they were concerned, they were not racist, nor had they done anything wrong! And to an extent, they would be right, because most quarky behaviour is unintentional. The thing is, it nonetheless reveals our true feelings.

When I was with Intel, I had been trying to arrange a meeting with the new General Manager and was in the office very early one morning. As I was walking along a corridor, I noticed him walking towards me. This was my chance to say hello, impress him that I was in the office so early and perhaps even secure a meeting with him.

As he walked towards me, I noticed that his face moved very slightly away from me and then as we got closer, fractionally away from me again, until he was almost looking out of the window. By this point I was alarmed – he was trying to avoid me. Who had been talking to him? I knew I could be a pain in the ass about leadership development but I was just being passionate. Who had I upset? By the time we crossed each other and he had completely ignored me, my career was in ruins and I was depressed for the rest of the day.

But what had just happened? If I had confronted him about it, he would probably have denied it and thought I was insane. How on earth could I describe what had just happened without seeming foolish? "Your face turned slightly away from me; you were avoiding me." He probably had no recollection of the incident. It was 7:15 in the morning, he was tired, distracted and something caught his eye outside the window ... or did it?

Quarkiness is ephemeral. Just as in quantum physics, the moment is here and gone in a microscopic flash. I was once giving a presentation in an auditorium and I noticed that the female presenter who preceded me got a wink from one of the directors before she started and then a supportive nod and a smile when she finished. My presentation was better, but I got no wink and no nod. I felt slightly depressed and distracted for the rest of the day, wondering if I had done anything wrong, or whether or not they were having a relationship!

Let's return to the choice that I made in Budapest. I recognised the quarkiness of the situation and how easy it would have been for me to emit a destructive barrage of strange quarks when I spotted the typing error. I smiled because I understood what was going on and the advantage that this gave me, because I was able to empower myself to be inspired by the error that I had witnessed.

Instead of doing harm, the error turned out to be a catalyst for a great day for an audience in Budapest and hopefully a better Chapter 5 in this book. I am smiling now as I share this story and feeling even more inspired as a result.

BITE 1

GET QUARKINESS ON THE RADAR

Eliminate corrosive negative micro-behaviours

You will not successfully eat the Elephant in the Room by confronting it, or attacking it, or telling it what to do. We need to creep up on the Elephant and create a climate that will ultimately be toxic for it.

Or, we can gently provide it with some tasty food for thought that will enable it to adapt to the new climate which we create.

At work, many of us, but especially our leaders, are too busy to do the right things. In fact, many leaders are frequently so busy, so tired and so stressed out, that it is no wonder they spend most of their time emitting waves of the strange quarks that are so destructive and corrosive.

What if we could have a better understanding of quarkiness and its key components?

Key Components of Quarkiness

1. Human beings constantly emit tiny manifestations of their disapproval or approval. I describe these manifestations as quarks.

2. Quarks generally take the form of body language, facial expressions, eye movements and sounds.

3. They are imperceptible, often unnoticed at a conscious level but are usually received sub-consciously.

4. They are frequently unintentional.

5. They betray our true feelings at some level.

6. The negative impact of strange quarks is cumulative and has a corrosive effect on engagement and results.

7. The positive impact of charms is proportionately greater.

8. In a typical meeting, hundreds of quarks are emitted, most of which are strange quarks.

9. Improving the relative proportion of charms will have a cosmic positive impact on engagement and results.

10. By getting quarkiness on the radar, we stand the best chance of success.

BITE TWO

Address the Three Terrible Triggers of Quarkiness

Eliminate the wrong kind of thinking about people

By making quarkiness visible and getting it into our corporate vocabulary, we have a chance to turn things around. Few leaders deliberately set out to have a destructive effect on their organisation, although many succeed. So if we can help them to reflect on an alternative approach that is more powerful and productive, why wouldn't they adopt it?

They're probably 'too busy'…

TERRIBLE TRIGGER 1

Silicon-Thinking

I mentioned earlier that Intel took the humble silicon chip and turned it into something quite extraordinary. In a business sense, this is simplistic, because what Intel achieved was quite incredible. Intel not only created amazing technology, which continues to provide the engine for most personal computing needs today, but they were able to accomplish production of the technology at a vast scale and with high quality.

My career with Intel was between 1990 and 2008 and in that time, I witnessed amazing technological advances, many of which were initiated by Intel. The company had rigorous manufacturing methods and some of the world's most complex processes, carried out in state of the art fabrication plants, containing massive clean rooms. The air that we breathe contains about 35 million particles per square metre that are bigger than 0.5 microns. By comparison an Intel clean room contains no more than a dozen particles per square metre, to a maximum size of 0.3 microns.

In order to achieve the amazing things that Intel has achieved, in silicon terms, the word 'flawless' was used a lot, along with the term 'defect-intolerant'. My issue with this is very simple. There are fundamental differences between Silicon and DNA and I feel that the silicon-thinking approach was excessively applied to the DNA of the organisation – in other words, people.

If you apply defect intolerance to your people, you will pay a heavy price over the long term. In my personal opinion, it felt like this kind of thinking manifested itself in Intel's performance management system, which on an annual basis, delivered hundreds of 'walking wounded' employees, who felt that they had been unfairly and subjectively judged by managers under pressure to meet performance distribution targets. It simply cannot be good for business to harm morale and engagement in such a manner.

Whilst I am critical about Intel's effectiveness in the area of performance management, my reflection on the matter is this – Intel missed a trick. If they had put the same amount of effort into developing and demanding the equivalent level of people management excellence as they did with technical excellence, I would have been a lot happier.

This is not about investing in high volumes of training, as Intel may claim. I know that investment in this area of development was reduced year after year. In any case, all the training in the world is meaningless if is felt by employees and new managers that application of the learning is not encouraged. I personally trained thousands of managers, but could not help feeling that few of them felt truly empowered to apply what they had learned back at work.

Remedy: Get this on the table, think differently about it and make a vow not to apply this kind of thinking to the DNA of the organisation.

TERRIBLE TRIGGER 2

Deficit-Thinking

During the Final Course of this book, Elephant Turnover, I will be looking at the flip-side of deficit-thinking. I describe it as Affirmative Thinking, which is a big bite of the Elephant in the Room. I cannot do this without first getting deficit-thinking on the table, which is a variation of silicon-thinking. It is also a key catalyst for the emission of strange quarks.

The deficit-thinking mind-set dictates that we are never good enough and if we apply a defect-intolerant approach as part of this thinking, we create the risk that certain well-intentioned approaches become ultimately damaging, especially when applied to the DNA side of organisations.

For example, the term 'continuous improvement' presupposes that we are never good enough. It stemmed from the work of William Edwards Deming (Total Quality) but it's a presupposition that can ultimately be a burden. I can live with continuous improvement, but the term that has really concerned me for many years is 'performance management'. Here, the presupposition is that many of our people are not good enough and must be identified, in order to be fixed or punished.

There is a thought leader on management and leadership that I admire greatly. He once said to me, "I don't like Intel's performance management system. Any system that results in thousands of walking wounded twice a year cannot be good for your business."

Remedy: Read about Affirmative Thinking in Chapter 8 then revisit this section. Make a fresh and radical decision about performance management in your organisation.

TERRIBLE TRIGGER 3

Theory X

Most people have forgotten about McGregor's theories of human motivation – Theory X and Theory Y. I think they are even more important today than when introduced in the 1960s. For now, I will just cover Theory X, which, despite empirical evidence that proves that it does not work, is alive and well in many large organisations today. All I ask you to do is to read my description, then reflect on current leadership issues that been foremost in the news in recent years – NHS scandals, Financial Services scandals and many more. It is essential that we either kill Theory X leaders, or urgently remove those who practise it.

Theory X managers and leaders operate on the presupposition that employees are inherently lazy, dislike work and will avoid responsibility whenever they can. This necessitates an incentive system to secure performance and if that doesn't work, then some kind of coercion is essential. Their thinking drives the belief that workers therefore need close supervision, with a comprehensive system of controls in place, such as performance management systems. Everything needs to be managed by a tight hierarchical structure, with narrow spans of control at all levels.

The climate that is created by Theory X managers and leaders is punitive, highly restrictive, with a culture of finger-pointing and blame and a complete lack of trust. Many Theory X managers and leaders are rewarded and promoted to more senior positions as a result of this approach.

Remedy: Read about Theory Y thinking in Chapter 8 and make it a critical business strategy to eradicate Theory X thinking from your organisation. Make it your mission to remove Theory X leaders for the good of your business.

Food for Thought

Think about this for a moment. Einstein's definition of insanity is all about doing the same thing over and over again but expecting a different result. Let me tell you a true story about performance management at Intel. As a manager who mistrusted the process, I always took the precaution of ensuring that I was better prepared than any other manager when we conducted our ranking and rating performance reviews. At Microsoft this was known as stack-ranking. Check out the 2012 Vanity Fair article in which all employees interviewed described stack-ranking as the most destructive process inside Microsoft.

One year at Intel I was criticised for failing to provide my quota of employees who were performing below expectations, despite being well prepared and able to back up my position that I had no poor performers that year. The next year, I was criticised for exceeding my quota of poor performers. As a result, another manager was off the hook and was thus able to tell one of his poor performers that he or she was actually a good performer after all. Was I the only person who appreciated the absurdity of the situation, this efficiently administered insanity?

I heard a rumour that Intel is currently reflecting upon its performance management system. I worry that this will end up being merely a long overdue process tweak, without a shift in the underlying process mentality that is too frequently used towards people and the far too often subjective assessments of their performance. I worked for Intel for eighteen years; I don't have an axe to grind with the organisation. Intel is amazing on the silicon side; I just want them to do a better job on the DNA side. I am still a share-holder and I expect better returns than I am getting on my investment.

CHAPTER 5: Summary and Final Thoughts

When I shared the Leader-hips story with you, I suggested that we have a choice to make when we respond to things that annoy us. We have the opportunity to be inspired by the typo or error, rather than being intolerant of it. Introducing the first of our four key words, Judging, I reassured you that our tendency to judge people who are different to us, typically with an air of disapproval, is based upon perfectly normal, predictable human behaviour. In other words, we all do it!

I suggested that you adopt my Standard Model of Quarkiness. That way, we can shift the balance, currently dominated by the sheer volume of negative micro-messages that we constantly emit towards each other, to the more positive micro-messages, or charms.

In order to accomplish such a worthy outcome, I suggested to you that we reject silicon-thinking (a defect-intolerant approach that is best suited to electronic chip manufacturing) as an attitude towards the DNA side of your organisation. I also suggested to you that we replace deficit-thinking, a belief that nothing is ever good enough, with affirmative thinking. Finally, I suggested that we remove Theory X believers from your organisation and replace them with Theory Y believers, who truly believe in the potential of people, your biggest asset.

We have finished our exploration of the word Judging, so let's move straight to Chapter 6, where we will look at the second key word, Understanding.

CHAPTER SIX

WELL-GRILLED Elephant

Q: How do you know there's an Elephant under your bed?

A: Your nose is touching the ceiling.

Normal Human Behaviour

I wish I could tell you that the quarkiness of Chapter 5 is odd or unusual. I'm afraid not. It's normal and, once understood, it's predictable and observable behaviour. This may seem like a comfort, but there is no escaping the cumulative damage done by the sheer volume of negative micro-messages that we send each other in the workplace every day, that is having such a corrosive effect on engagement, morale and performance.

So what happens as we start to understand what's going on? Well, the answer is that amazing things can happen.

My own work on leadership and team behaviour has been indirectly inspired by the work of Carl Jung, who famously separated from his mentor Sigmund Freud in 1913, partly because of fundamental differences in opinion about the relationship between sexual development and libido on core personality. (I will leave that topic for others to cover.)

One interpretation of this is that Jung tended towards the study of more normal human behaviour, and indeed his work in this space inspired much of the good work done in behavioural science during the 20th century, including the Myers-Briggs and DISC behavioural tools that I use.

I will return to the area of human behaviour soon, but before I do, let me tell you a very important story, which leads us into our third bite of the Elephant.

Lessons from rats

One of my favourite stories is about rats. There was a Harvard University professor called Robert Rosenthal and one day he gathered his students together with an interesting assignment. He wanted them to collect conclusive empirical evidence about the relative performance of two different strains of rat. He assigned half of the students to observe and measure the performance of a group of super-bright Maze Rats. The other half of his students were assigned a group of pretty stupid Dull Rats.

The results and data provided by the two groups of students were considerable and conclusive.

The analysis and evidence provided by the first group of students proved without any doubt that the Maze Rats were really bright rats. When the students were asked how they felt about working with these rats, they found it to be a pleasant experience.

The analysis and evidence provided by the second group of students was also conclusive. It proved without any doubt that the Dull Rats were really stupid rats. When the students were asked how they felt about working with these rats, they found it to be a rather unpleasant experience. Please note once again – the results and data provided by the two groups of students were considerable and conclusive. Rosenthal then dropped the bombshell that both groups had been working with the same rats.

The purpose of his study had nothing to do with the need for empirical evidence about the relative performance of two, non-existent, rat types. On the contrary, the study was all about something that he called Self-Fulfilling Prophecy.

BITE THREE

Get Self-Fulfilling Prophecy onto the Corporate Radar

It's time to change your filters

The rats that Rosenthal provided to his students were the same rats, so the only thing that was different for them was the expectation that they had been given about the performance of the rats. Based upon these expectations the students were able to provide a significant amount of supporting evidence – either way.

The same thing happens when we apply the concept of self-fulfilling prophecy to human beings. People will live up or down to our expectations.

Here's what happens:

1. We form certain expectation of people or events. When we look at others do we see a Maze Rat or a Dull Rat?

2. We communicate these expectations by transmitting a variety of cues, e.g. Standard Model of Quarkiness.

3. People respond to these cues by adjusting their behaviour to match them.

4. The outcome is that the original expectation becomes true.

When we have self-fulfilling prophecies in place regarding others, we create two sets of filters. If our expectations are positive, in addition to sending out positive cues that influence our expected outcome, we put in place the filter that filters out all of the bad stuff, so that only the good stuff remains. This reinforces our beliefs about that person. I wonder how much of this happens when we make decisions about who to promote into senior leadership positions?

If our expectations are negative, we will find that we are not disappointed! This time, in addition to sending out myriad negative cues, we put in place the filter that filters out all of the good stuff so that only the bad stuff remains, thus proving our negative expectations about that person. I wonder how much of this happens during performance reviews, or how many careers have been ruined as a result? It's a sobering thought.

UNDERSTANDING

Are you noticing the parallels between self-fulfilling prophecy and judging? If a person is different from us, we may form a series of unwarranted expectations about that person which cause us to behave in the way that we do.

What if we could truly understand what was going on?

If I succeed in helping you to understand what is going on, I know that you will be able to see the Elephant in the Room. We will have a common perspective and a common language that enables us to talk about the Elephant with others and to get the unspoken truth on the table.

What if the Elephant is you?

None of us are excluded from the definition of 'normal human behaviour'. There are many big words that come to mind when we describe the Elephant in the Room and one of those words is 'denial'. This is all part of the unspoken truth that saturates the atmosphere in which the Elephant thrives.

It is vital that you digest the following nugget of food for thought before we move deeper into the subject. The thought is this – if Judging is one of the critical elements that injects oxygen into the climate that enables the Elephant in the Room to exist, then Understanding is the door through which we need to walk in order to build a different climate, one which is fuelled by Appreciating and Valuing, which we will cover in Chapters 8 and 9.

Our basic premise is that most of the factors that have led to the existence of the Elephant in the Room are ultimately driven by normal, predictable human behaviour. You are not going to change just because somebody like me tells you that you must.

For most of us, part of our behavioural makeup is that we do not like to be told what to do. Therefore, if I can work with you to find a way to help you to open your eyes to what is going on and why, (not just for you but for others as well), then that fresh understanding will mean that you will never look at yourself, or other people, in the same way ever again. It will be impossible to deny this new understanding, but most importantly, it will be your decision to do something with it, for the simple reason that it has become so completely obvious to you. It's a no-brainer.

Self-Awareness

Daniel Goleman was very influential in bringing the concept of Emotional Intelligence (1995) to the table in his first book. Since then, the relationship between emotional intelligence and great leadership has been powerfully established. At its most simple level, emotional intelligence (EI) has three simple aspects:

1. Self-awareness
2. Awareness of the needs of other people
3. Adapting your style by using this new awareness in a productive way that enhances your relationships with others.

In bringing EI to the table, Daniel Goleman also brought it to the heart of leadership. There are varying opinions about how effective he was in showing us how to become more emotionally intelligent. One wonders about the number of occasions where attempts have been made to fix leaders who lacked emotional intelligence by simply sending them on some kind of emotional intelligence workshop, with the expectation of an immediate result.

If it's that important, maybe the sensible approach is to invest effort into making sure that you make the right leadership selection decisions, rather than waiting until after the event, in the hope that you can repair the damage caused by a bad decision. Of course, if it was that easy we would all be doing it.

What has absorbed me in my leadership work is the 'how'. How can I help people (and not just those with a problem in their already occupied senior positions) to develop increasing levels of EI over time? How can I help you without patronising you, boring you, telling you what to do, or bombarding you with yet more leadership theory? It has become somewhat of a mission.

This focus on the 'how' necessitates an outcome-driven approach on my part. Rather than just creating a cool, interesting workshop and hoping for the best, most of the work that I do with teams, as well as with managers and leaders, focuses on how to achieve emotional intelligence as a somewhat longer term outcome.

EI does not appear overnight and it will never appear if we keep providing the same old fare to our future leaders. My belief is as follows. If we are able to keep the over-arching outcome in mind at all times (and know our stuff) then bit by bit (or rather, bite by bite) we will progress inevitably towards that outcome.

EQ versus IQ

Emotional Intelligence (EI) is sometimes described as Emotional Quotient (EQ) in order to distinguish it from Intellectual Quotient (IQ). In Financial Services, there are many people, mostly male, in senior leadership positions, who possess high IQs. They are armed with first class honours degrees in subjects like mathematics from universities such as Oxford and Cambridge, or MBAs from Harvard, Yale and other Ivy League universities. Big players in Financial Services and other large corporations vie for their services, offering huge financial incentives and a fast-track onto the upper echelons of their new employer's leadership pipeline.

Some of you may have heard such high-IQ senior managers described as 'cone-heads', an affectionate term which implies that their people skills and inter-personal skills are not quite as mature or advanced as their academic skills. Yet they continue to be in demand and continue their rapid upward trajectory in the organisation. Over the years, I have met a few who had great people skills. They were amazing, but very rare.

Of course, the sixty-four thousand dollar question is can we take an academically gifted person with a high IQ and improve their EQ? The answer is a qualified yes. Read on...

BITE FOUR

Know the Colour of the Elephant

To know the Elephant is to help the Elephant

I am going to ask you to trust me for the next few pages. This is a tried and tested approach that I use with groups of people and I'm really excited to be using it just with you.

Please stand up in the middle of the room and face the window or TV, ideally in an empty room with a bit of space to move around. The window or TV is the front of the room.

Now, imagine that there is a horizontal line running from right to left along the middle of the room. You are standing in the middle of that line. We will call this line your Relative Pace.

In a moment you are going to make a decision to move along that line, from your current position in the middle of the room, to your left, or your right, in order to find a point on this line that you feel represents the relative pace, or speed, at which you operate, compared to that of other people you know.

In life, we all operate at different speeds. This is perfectly natural, normal and observable. Think about people that you know well, including family members. In order to make your decision, there are just two options, which are:

Slower Pace: As you look to your right, think about people who take a more deliberate, cautious approach to their work and life. For example, they may need a little longer to make decisions. They are more accurate and thoughtful. At the extreme end of the line, where they are up against the wall, they could be extremely slow, indecisive and hesitant about change and new ideas.

Faster Pace: As you now look to your left, think about people you know who are generally quicker witted, physically faster and more reactive, less cautious and more decisive in their approach to work and life. A person standing at the extreme end of this line might be regarded by others as reckless, over-hasty and possibly even out of control. They will overlook details in their haste.

Now reflect on your own relative pace. Before you move, remember the following rules:

1. There is no right answer. Please be honest. I'm the only other person in the room with you and I promise I will not tell anyone. The honest answer is the right answer.

2. Faster is not necessarily better. Sometimes, people assume that faster is better, probably for reasons associated with the Elephant in the Room, and feel that they ought to move to their left. The honest answer is the right answer.

3. You cannot stay where you are. You must make a decision. Left or right?

4. Can't make up your mind? If you were faster paced, can you understand why making a decision on this would not be a problem for you? You should move towards your right.

Now move either to your right or to your left until you reach a point along the line that you feel is right for you. I usually find that most people are very honest about this. This is great because it also means that they are making an accurate diagnosis of their relative pace.

Now imagine that there is a vertical line running along the middle of the room, bisecting the horizontal line on which you are standing. This is the line of Relative Focus and is based upon your personal orientation towards just two things – people and tasks. Your options therefore are:

Move Backwards: Your task or goal orientation is stronger for you than your people orientation. The further backwards you move, slowly and observing good health and safety precautions, the less people focus, or people skills, you believe that you have, relative to your focus on tasks. If you find that you are nudging the wall, you really do admit to not being that much of a people person. One such person admitted to me that he preferred things to people. I admired his honesty.

Move Forwards: The further forwards you move the stronger your people orientation is compared with your focus on tasks and goals. This is not saying that you're not committed. It's merely an honest reflection of your relative focus. If you move a little bit forward from the middle, you are saying that your task focus remains fairly high, just not as high as your people focus. If you find that you are nudging the TV or the window, your people focus is extremely important to you, to a significantly greater extent than your goal or task focus.

Please move forwards or backwards now; as before, there is no right or wrong answer. The right answer is the honest answer. In order to get to the real you and to properly develop your growing diagnostic capability, it is essential that you are honest and move backwards or forwards. Please make a note of the point where you are standing.

Now, pick somebody at work that you know really well. Imagine that they are in the room with you and repeat the same diagnosis for them that you have just used on yourself. Please note my use of the word 'diagnosis' here because as you do it, you are developing a skill. What is their relative pace? Is it similar to you or different? What is their relative focus? Is it more people-oriented or more task-focused?

Please make a decision about their relative focus and make a note of the point that they would be standing in the room, relative to you. You have just made a pretty accurate diagnosis.

If you were to now separate the room into four quadrants, separated by the horizontal and vertical lines, you will find that you are standing inside one of them. They are:

BLUE Slower Task Focus	**RED** Faster Task Focus
GREEN Slower People Focus	**YELLOW** Faster People Focus

I have assigned a colour to each of the four quadrants of the room and we will explore the reason in a moment. First return to the person you know well. Are they in the same quadrant as you? If not, I'll bet that they are in an adjacent quadrant. I'm willing to bet that they are not in a quadrant that is diagonally opposite to you.

What I have just shared is simple. It's also at the heart of behavioural science. Most human behaviour is normal, as well as observable and predictable. I use two behavioural tools – DISC and Myers-Briggs – but have a personal preference for the former because I can easily teach the diagnostic skills to other people. Using DISC I can help teams to make massive strides in improving relationships and much more besides.

Let me explain how DISC relates to the exercise that you have just completed. For each colour, starting with red, think of a few emotions or other words that you would associate with each colour. As you do so, think about your colour; do you associate these words with yourself? What about the other person in the room?

The words you think of might include the following:

Red   Anger, Danger, Passion (D)

Yellow   Cheerful, Bright, Sunny (I)

Green   Caring, Calm, Safe (S)

Blue   Cold, Aloof, Clear (C)

DISC is an acronym, each letter relating to one of the four colours listed above. Now think of three words beginning with D that relate to Red; think of three I words for Yellow and so on.

You might get some of these words:

Red   Dominant, Directive, Driver

Yellow   Influential, Inspiring, Ingenious

Green   Steady, Safe, Sensible

Blue   Compliant, Cool, Calculating

For DISC, the four descriptors are Dominance (Red), Influence (Yellow), Steadiness (Green) and Compliance (Blue).

BLUE Compliance	**RED** Dominance
GREEN Steadiness	**YELLOW** Influence

Red: (Dominance)

Are you starting to see how a fast-paced, task-focused person can be dominant, single minded, impatient and even hot-tempered? They like to be busy, keeping a lot of balls in the air, and are not good listeners. They are valued for their single minded focus on getting the work done, but they will rely on others to clear up the mess that they leave behind in their pursuit of personal success.

Reds can also be self-centred and egotistical. They thrive on recognition, so you can usually identify a Red desk at work, firstly by the various recognition awards that are visibly displayed, and secondly by the mess. If a Red asks you how you are, it's just words to them and they are not that interested in your reply.

Communication tip: Beware if you fail to quickly get to the point with Reds. Stick to business.

Yellow: (Influence)

People who are fast-paced and people-focused tend to be very bright, optimistic, gregarious and almost certainly extroverted. They may be quite animated and can be infectious in their enthusiasm, hence the influence and ability to inspire others; but they do love to talk, which of course means that Yellows may also be poor listeners. This is not because they are not interested in people. Far from it; however the sheer volume of ideas that bounce around in their heads can get in the way and be a major distraction.

Yellows are also much happier sharing their ideas and talking about their ideas than listening. They can be somewhat egotistical, but for different reasons than Reds. Yellows, however, are the most likely to trust people and will feel most comfortable in delegating and empowering others. This in part is why they can be so influential and inspirational to work with.

Their sense of humour and ability to quickly develop friendships is a powerful mix and their balanced approach to decision-making is also effective. They do need to be more organised though, and one sign of a Yellow desk is the stacks of paper on it. They can also get emotional and verbally cutting under pressure, so watch out for that too and be ready with a warm word and a supportive arm around their shoulder. They just want to be loved.

Communication tip: Be warm and friendly and don't get bogged down with detail when you work with Yellows. Don't be abrupt or try to control the conversation. Give them space to talk.

Green: (Steadiness)

People who are slower-paced and people-focused tend to genuinely care about other people along with the environment in which they live and work.

If a Green asks you how you are, unlike a Red, they will be genuinely interested in your answer and will listen carefully to it. They are great listeners. They are also friendly and supportive, with a strong desire to support and serve others – something we may take too much advantage of, along with their good nature.

Greens are stable, consistent and reliable. They maintain a calm composed disposition and can concentrate on the task in hand until it is completed. This compelling mix of being a reliable team player who will complete what they have started is of great value to the organisation. On the other hand, their lack of urgency can be frustrating at times, as is their reliance on routines and resistance to change.

They are the most likely colour to be sweeping up after Reds and we do need to ensure that they are not excessively dominated by others, because they do find it terribly difficult to say no.

Communication tip: Show personal interest before getting down to business with Greens. Adopt a non-threatening demeanour. Ask 'how' to draw out their ideas, opinions and feelings, especially about change.

Blue: (Compliance)

For this colour, when we use the word compliance it has a different meaning to the kind of compliance that is demonstrated by Greens when the Reds are ganging up on them, trying to get their way.

Quality and accuracy is like oxygen to Blues. They have high standards when it comes to doing things right and backing up their opinions with facts and figures. They will be very judgemental of others who do not – for example, Yellows. Their compliance descriptor comes from their strict adherence to policies and procedures. They can be described as analytical and the discipline that they demonstrate can be exceedingly valuable in certain types of organisation. Finance perhaps?

In relationships, Blues are described as diplomatic. This may seem surprising, but it is not because they are good with people. It is because they realise that building relationships is difficult for them and any kind of rules, traditions or protocol will be very helpful. Their interpersonal style may come across as clipped and even careful, because they don't want to get it wrong. Projects may get bogged down by Blue team members and their need for perfection.

Communication tip: Do not be casual, messy or disorganised in your approach with Blues. Be specific and back up what you say with facts. Be prepared for a stern look in reply if you use phrases like 'big picture' with a Blue.

I strongly recommend taking the time to understand DISC and how it works. For Elephant-eating purposes, it really helps when you have enough understanding to enable you to appreciate the differences between the four colours. I would also stress that your ideal behavioural style is a blend of at least two colours. That way, one colour balances the other. If your blend is extremely biased towards just one colour, this can make life more challenging for you and for others, especially if that extreme colour is red.

Here is a summary with a few key attributes of the four colours:

RED	Attributes
Personal Goals:	Dominance and independence
Basis for Judging others:	Their speed of task completion
Method of Influence:	Directive, forceful, controlling
Value to Organisations:	Their can-do attitude
Potential Impact:	Can be blunt, intense and aggressive

YELLOW	Attributes
Personal Goals:	To help others and build relationships
Basis for Judging others:	Their warmth
Method of Influence:	Interpersonal skills and enthusiasm
Value to Organisations:	Pulls people towards a vision
Potential Impact:	Can be emotional and verbose

GREEN	Attributes
Personal Goals:	Stability, dependability and security
Basis for Judging others:	Their consistency and reliability
Method of Influence:	Supportive approach and pleasant attitude
Value to Organisations:	A stable, reliable team player
Potential Impact:	Lack of urgency, inability to say no

BLUE	Attributes
Personal Goals:	Quality, accuracy and order
Basis for Judging others:	Their own standards of accuracy and facts
Method of Influence:	Use of data and facts to support their case
Value to Organisations:	High standards, discipline and data
Potential Impact:	Inflexible, critical, do things 'by the book'

So what colour is the Elephant in the Room?

Blue? If the Elephant in the Room is blue, the organisation may get so wrapped up in policies, procedures and data that it becomes totally bureaucratic. An organisation like this will not be fast-moving. Key strategic decisions may take an age to be made, during which time the competition are eating your lunch, and projects may constantly miss deadlines because of the need for quality and accuracy.

A culture may emerge where people are critiqued in the same way as systems as procedures are. Such a culture may end up as being unhealthily defect-intolerant.

Green? If the Elephant in the Room is green, the organisation may become suffocated by a caring culture where rapid change is impossible and once again, faster-paced, more decisive competitors outwit you in the marketplace. Deadlines will be missed because of the need to involve everybody and ensure that they are listened to, but the feel-good factor will be high. Or will it?

Faster-paced employees will become increasingly frustrated at the inability of the organisation to get things done and eventually the reds will either win or leave.

Yellow? If the Elephant in the Room is yellow, this is going to be a fun place to work. People are trusted and empowered to make decisions and many good ideas fly through the air in this creative, innovative environment. People will constantly gather around flipcharts to write the latest mission statement and animatedly discuss their latest ideas.

If only they would shut up they might actually accomplish some of the great ideas, but they love to talk. Blues will stand on the edges, shaking their heads in frustration, because Yellows are frequently unrealistic, they never provide hard evidence to support their ideas, and nothing tangible is being accomplished. They are just too casual and disorganised.

Most Elephant in the Room issues tend to emerge as the result of a lack of people focus, so the Blues merit closer attention. However, Blues do tend to realise their shortcomings on the people side, and as long as you meet them halfway and meet their needs, they will reciprocate in their own diplomatic way.

The colour that we need to focus on in a lot more detail is **red**. Let's do that in Chapter 7 and then make some comparisons with the big Elephant issues that we discussed in earlier chapters.

CHAPTER 6 – Summary and Final Thoughts

Having explored our first key word, Judging, in Chapter 5, we moved to our second key word, Understanding. This is the next critical step that takes us further towards appreciating and valuing each other.

What we are talking about is based on normal, predictable, observable human behaviour. I talked about the importance of self-awareness as part of our dining strategy. The ability to understanding ourselves and each other better is a key ingredient of success. Understanding the four colours of human behaviour gives us valuable resources in responding to the needs of people who are different to us.

Who would have thought that rats could provide us with so much food for thought? In looking at the work of Robert Rosenthal on self-fulfilling prophecy, we realised that people will live up or down to the expectations that we form about them. We will make sure that this happens by sending out cues that drive people's behaviour to ensure that our expectations become true. We will also put appropriate filters in place which guarantee that our expectations are always met, even if they are totally wrong.

Our mission is to get the unspoken truth into plain sight and onto the table. In the case of the Elephant, an acute lack of people focus (or worse, poor behaviour towards people) is at the heart of it. That is why our work on understanding human behaviour and, in particular, the colour red, is not yet complete.

How to Eat the Elephant in the Room

CHAPTER SEVEN

Elephant IN FIERY HOT RED SAUCE

Q: What do you call an Elephant with a Machine Gun?

A: Sir!

The next few pages build on the work that we did in Chapter 6 and explore in depth the premise that the Elephant in the Room is primarily red, or has evolved for red reasons. They contain a behavioural analysis of the extreme red style and compare it to some key criteria for effective leadership. This analysis is then followed by some important recommendations for those of us who have an extreme red behavioural style.

As a master practitioner in the DISC behavioural tool, I use DISC in a variety of ways in my work with teams, managers and leaders; and also in my work as an executive coach. It is, in my opinion, the most simple, user-friendly, powerful and effective tool available to my clients. In the right hands, it can also be used to assist clients in their decision-making processes with respect to effective leadership development.

Frequently, poor decisions are made with respect to the identification of future leadership potential. Two of the key drivers of individual performance – task competence and execution – are NOT the best overall indicators of future leadership potential. Expertise plus Hard Work does not equal Leadership.

In his book 'The Leadership Pipeline', Ram Charan (et al) expresses the mantra "Get the right people on the bus". His five signs of a misplaced manager of managers are:

1. An inability to delegate

2. Poor performance management

3. Failure to build a strong team

4. A single minded focus on getting the work done

5. Choosing clones over contributors.

There is a high probability that many extreme Reds who are in leadership positions will exhibit these behaviours. I can think of occasions where advice was ignored about extreme red candidates for senior positions. Frequently, major issues quickly emerged about their leadership capability, and relationship issues quickly developed with other colleagues.

Let's have a look at the typical traits of an extreme Red.

EXTREME RED = EXTREME DANGER

As you read earlier, the behavioural characteristics of an extreme Red are extremely fast pace and very high task focus, with very low people focus. The extreme Red leader is often described as 'The Autocrat'. Their highly dominant profile exhibits high levels of assertiveness and a need for control, demonstrating a capacity to be domineering, intimidating and overbearing at times.

This type of person has a very high need to achieve and because of this they are highly ambitious and competitive, striving aggressively to achieve their goals. Their fast pace brings with it a dynamic and decisive nature which in certain circumstances can be eye-catching. But their tendency to juggle many balls in the air, allied to a somewhat reckless approach at times, can leave a trail of mess for other colleagues to clean up, while they single mindedly pursue their personal objectives.

Extreme Reds and Relationships

The extreme Red's emphasis on achievement and personal success may significantly affect their relationships with other people. In extreme cases, they will treat other colleagues simply as a means to an end, or a way of achieving their personal goals. They will typically have a blind-spot when it comes to the feelings of others and because of their dominant style people will hesitate to give them feedback, which they so badly need.

Their highly competitive nature can be destructive, because they are naturally suspicious and sceptical, seeing challenges and opposition everywhere. They are seen by others as self-serving. Their need to win and to be right may even mean that they end up competing with subordinates on minor decisions that they should be delegating! In fact, they find true delegation and empowerment very difficult, almost pathologically so.

Extreme Reds and Leadership

In the long run, placing an extreme Red in a leadership position is such a high risk that it could end up being catastrophic for the organisation. If we look at many of the problems and scandals that have emerged in the media in the past few years, Reds have damaged the reputations of many organisations in Financial Services, the NHS and others, where allegations of bullying have too frequently turned out to be true.

In addition to well-documented behaviours such as bullying, self-serving leadership has often been described as a common theme behind the chronic failures in these organisations. It is my belief that many of these failures have occurred and grown more acute over time as a result of placing extreme Reds in leadership positions without carrying out the due diligence needed to confirm their suitability for the role.

Daniel Goleman outlined two leadership styles – Commanding and Pace-Setting – which have the most damaging effect on organisations. Yet it is these very styles that are rewarded today with promotions into increasingly more senior leadership positions. Extreme Reds in leadership positions are often 'too busy' to perform key aspects of their roles, such as developing people. Their diaries are probably clogged up with 1:1s with board members who they think can help them to further advance their careers.

Ultimately, think twice before promoting an extreme Red into a leadership position, as the odds are that it will end badly for the organisation.

Three RED Words

Results: Extreme Reds will single mindedly and impatiently pursue results that fuel their highly competitive nature and need for personal success. Yes, results are important, but others may have to clear up the mess that they leave behind!

Ego: Extreme Reds put their own needs ahead of others and in DISC work, they honestly believe that red is the best colour. They are impatient to succeed and may invest an inordinate amount of time influencing upwards in order to accelerate their desired upward trajectory in the organisation.

Dominance: This is the D in DISC and extreme Reds can be perceived as autocratic. Their need for power may be acute. Their need to control, to win and to be right can put them at odds with colleagues, even with subordinates. They are consistently decisive, even if they are wrong.

What if the Elephant in the Room is YOU?

If your behavioural style is extreme red and you are in a leadership position, then you may very well have contributed to the prevailing environment and culture of your organisation, but not in a good way. The chances are that the conversations that people in your team are having about you are not the type of conversations that you would feel comfortable hearing.

Let's be blunt and get to the point, because we know this works for you. The potential damage that you are doing to your organisation is significant. This may very well be a surprise to you, because people are reluctant to give you feedback. You may also be starting to feel angry. This is a predictable reaction from an extreme Red. Sorry, it's not good news.

BITE FIVE

Provide Self-Help for Red Elephants

Red Elephants kill organisations

If you have an extreme red behavioural style, please read this. If you know anybody who has an extreme red style, make sure that they receive a copy of this – urgently.

Constantly seek and act on feedback

Consult a true cross-section of colleagues, especially across and down, then listen carefully to what they say because it will be the truth that you hear. Do you find that you get into your default defensive position, disagreeing with the feedback? Think about why you are disagreeing with the truth, realise that feedback is a gift, then show respect for the feedback by responding positively to it, even if you find it hard. The more you ask for feedback and act on it the easier it gets. Never disrespect people who give you the gift of feedback.

Swallow your pride

Finger-pointing and blaming others will damage your reputation far more quickly than any mistakes or poor decisions that you make. It is impossible for you to be right all the time. If you're in the wrong, put your hand up, admit it, then apologise and demonstrate your sincerity. "I screwed up" are three very powerful words. "I'm sorry" is also powerful. Try it. Sorry is not the hardest word.

Trust your team and treat everyone as equals

Recognise that your team has just as much to contribute as you individually and a huge amount more collectively. Appreciate their strengths, consider their ideas and once you have created a solution together, trust and empower them to share the load, without constant interference from you. You're their manager, not their messiah – they'll be fine. In fact, the odd mistake is a great learning opportunity. Feel comfortable about delegating to others – yes it's hard for somebody like you, but it is mission-critical if you want to succeed as a leader. Trust arrives on foot, but departs in a Ferrari.

Go for gold, not glory

Or as Mike Abrashoff said in his book: "It's your ship – focus on results – not salutes!" Leaders who avoid the glare of the spotlight tend to be more successful. Give your obsession with status a rest and let your results, or more importantly, the results of your team, speak for you as the leader of the team. Think about the responsibility that you have as a leader to the organisation, to upholding its values and to creating the right environment for the kind of success where everybody wins and not just you. It's not all about you!

Stop fishing for compliments

Trying constantly to convince people senior to you that you're the best thing since sliced bread? Grow up! People have better things to do than massage your ego. Let pride in your work fuel your confidence. Try fishing for compliments at home. You will probably get more positive stokes the less hard you seek them. Leave your ego in the car park when you arrive at work.

Let others shine

Seek opportunities to allow members of your team to demonstrate just how talented they are. Take pride in their success and publicly praise their contributions, naming them and being specific about how they excelled, as well as how you feel about it. People are more generous with their time and support when they believe they'll be appreciated. They may even reciprocate. Stop competing with your team and share the credit!

Be selfless, not selfish

Believe it or not, people in your team have needs as well. They are not simply a means to an end in achieving your personal career goals. If someone asks for personal advice, put your own agenda to one side. Coach them, listen to what they are saying and base your advice and guidance on what you genuinely think will help them to be successful. This will make you more successful as a result. Winning leaders are those who invest time in developing their team and having regular meaningful career discussions with them. Put your people first. You might get to like it.

Be patient

Just joined as the superstar fast-tracker? Heading for the top in 2 to 3 years? Telling anybody who will listen? I repeat – grow up! Don't expect instant respect. It can take many years to build the kind of leadership that convinces board members that you have the right calibre. Respect the culture. You are entitled to nothing yet. Rome wasn't built in a day – neither is your reputation.

Be vulnerable

It is strategically sound to reveal your imperfections. The greatest leaders are never afraid to be fallible or vulnerable. They go to the loo just like the rest of us! I suggest that you check out Brené Brown's TED talk on vulnerability. Look in the mirror – what do other people see? Nobody›s perfect – especially not you.

BITE SIX

The Two Chasms

Get the right people on the bus

We are going to take a short break from colours so we can spend some time looking at leadership, but we will return later in order to explore all four colours from a leadership point of view.

It is an undeniable fact that at the heart of the big deep-rooted issues in organisations – the unspoken truth that masks seismic fissures in the culture – is a combination of poor leadership and quite unacceptable behaviour. This is the kind of appalling behaviour towards others which disrespects and damages the DNA of organisations – the people – without whom organisations cannot exist, let alone flourish and compete effectively.

Why do behaviours that are empirically proven to guarantee failure get rewarded? This further pollutes the culture and potential of so many organisations. It beggars belief.

We can complain for another twenty years, or we can do something about it, starting now. The first step is to take a fairly simplistic look at the journey from the bottom of an organisation towards the top and look at what typically happens compared to what should happen, and then act. Our journey has just four points (or levels) on it, with deep chasms between levels 2 and 3 and between levels 3 and 4.

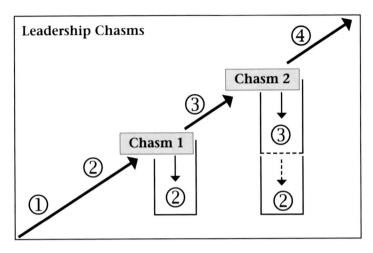

Level 1: Entry Level Contributor

Level 2: Performer

DEEP CHASM

Level 3: Manager

DEEPER CHASM

Level 4: Leader

If you fall into a deep chasm in normal life, your life is probably over, with every bone in your body smashed to smithereens. It's a pretty high impact event, with bloody consequences for you. Something similar happens in this scenario.

How do you cross a chasm? Well, you can try jumping, but it's quite a distance. You could build a bridge I suppose. That might work, but you would need to successfully get somebody across to the other side in order to help. Either way, it's not easy; however we will talk more about how to cross chasms when we reach the first one.

In all organisations, many people start from the bottom, at Entry

Level. For an average employee things are going to be pretty new for them and it will take them some time to become familiar with the tasks that they are expected to perform and to get to know their fellow workers.

Frequently we may give new employees a six month probationary period to get up to speed and start earning their salary in full. In other words, our expectations about their performance and contribution will be low at first.

Characteristics of Level 1:

- Low level of competence
- Lack of familiarity with the organisation
- Low expectations about their performance
- High initial dependence on direction and support
- Typical duration: 6 months.

After a relatively short period of time, when the necessary skills, experience and confidence have been gained, they are admitted to the ranks of their fellow workers, moving up to the next level, which is Performer.

Expectations about employees' performance will continue to increase over time and they will be rewarded according to their relative contribution, perhaps moving through a number of increasingly more senior grades, commensurate with their experience and resultant value to the organisation.

They will contribute effectively as part of the team and, depending on their performance, they may be identified as future management potential. They will get opportunities to demonstrate their developing management skills by managing small projects, or deputising for the boss.

Characteristics of Level 2:

- Competence and performance expectations grow
- Knows the organisation
- Solves problems well
- Works well with others as part of a team
- Self-reliant with a low need for direction or support
- Takes responsibility for their own development
- Typical duration: could be their entire career.

For some Level 2 Performers, we are now standing at the edge of the first chasm. To be successful at the next level, that of being a Manager, it is imperative that the Performer understands the need to 'let go'. This is very difficult, even for Performers with strong people focus, because it requires them to let go of the very attributes that made them successful as a Level 2 Performer. It is so hard that it can be psychologically difficult.

A key component of a successful transition to the Level 3 Manager position is the ability to work effectively through others, who are now accountable to you for their contribution. The nature of your work has changed. You are no longer the fast track Performer who worked harder and longer than your peers. They now look to you for direction and support. Your boss, who promoted you, looks to you to get all of the work done, this time by a larger number of people than just yourself.

But what if these new expectations were never clearly explained to you? Or what if you ignored them, preferring to carry on in the same way as you did before? If it's any comfort to you, you are probably in a majority of people who fail to effectively make the transition.

Research shows that the relative value of your contribution as a Performer has the potential to increase significantly, compared to others in the same role, as you progress upwards in the organisation. Given that we typically represent leadership progression as a straight 45 degree line, I have, for the purposes of this discussion, developed some simple indicators which I believe provide an appropriate and pretty credible comparison of relative value to the organisation.

The potential value of your results to the organisation:

Contributor: This grows to about 15%

Performer: In line with contribution, it doubles to 30%

Manager: This can double again to 60% but...

CHASM 1 - DEEP CHASM

If you fail to effectively make the transition from high Performer to Manager, your potential value to the organisation takes a nose dive in value from 60% to 20%, just above that of an entry level Contributor.

This is a disaster for you, for the organisation and almost certainly for the people that you are supposed to be supporting. They will become increasingly frustrated by your obsession with work and your lack of direction and support. Your reputation, your value to the organisation, the morale of the team, and much more besides, has plummeted into a deep hole. And as you get busier and are forced to work longer and harder to see that the work gets done – because you are trying to do so much of it yourself – you get more tired, more stressed and start to behave like people under stress behave – irrationally.

Characteristics of Level 3:

- Works and delivers results through others
- Sets goals which connect to the work people do
- Coaches, develops and motivates team members
- Provides direction and support as required
- Co-operates well across different functions.

Many managers frequently complain that they are 'too busy' to exhibit the very attributes that will double their value to the organisation. Instead, they fail to make the transition from high performing Contributor to Manager, expecting that they will continue to be rewarded. We now know that this makes no business sense.

An effective manager may once again catch the eye of someone above and be identified as having leadership potential. Expectations once again change and if the Manager successfully makes the transition to Leader, their relative value to the organisation increases once more to as much as 90%. This is huge.

Let's look at their new requirements as a Leader. The primary role of the Manager is to ensure that the work of their team gets done to the agreed-upon level of quality and within the required timescales. Stephen R Covey put it nicely when he summarised a key part of their responsibility as 'PC versus P' or focus on 'Production Capability' rather than just 'Production'.

We frequently talk about the need for leaders to be more strategic and less tactical. This implies a greater focus on the 'why', the purpose and outcome of the work, rather than the 'what', the completion of the work itself.

We also talk about the need for many of our leaders to be better at decision making. This is important, because leaders not only make decisions but, depending upon their position, they make decisions which are consequential. In other words, the decisions that they make will have a material effect on the future of the organisation.

There is a lot more besides that you can do as a leader that will ensure your relative contribution and value to the organisation is at the 90% mark. In Chapter 9, I will be sharing my GIVE approach to leadership. Don't miss it.

As an effective Manager reflects on their leadership ambitions, they are standing at the edge of a second deep chasm. Whether or not they fall in depends completely upon their ability to demonstrate the attributes of a Level 4 Leader.

Characteristics of Level 4:

- Is strategic and makes wise balanced decisions

- Thinks and acts positively; energises others

- Is self-aware, not self-promoting

- Invests time in identifying and developing talent

- Puts the company and its people first.

There is a strategic time horizon which dictates the scope of a Leader's responsibilities. The horizon for Levels 1 to 3 may range from as little as one day or one shift to a week or a month, perhaps even a quarter. Leaders look much further ahead – one year, three years, five years or more – because they need to be able to anticipate and respond to new and changing competitive realities. They also need to make sure that their organisation can adapt to changing social, legal, political and financial circumstances.

Leaders cannot accomplish the above if they continue to be

absorbed by short-term tactical, transactional or work-related matters that should be dealt with by people further down their organisation.

CHASM 2 – DEEPER CHASM

If you fail to make the transition from Manager to Leader, the first problem for you is the missed opportunity of failing to achieve a further 30% increase in your value to the organisation.

The second problem, caused by you, will be the probability that you will now interfere with decisions and with activity that should be performed by people further down the organisation.

Third will be the loss of critical time being productively spent on leadership work because you are 'too busy' getting involved in creating the previous problem.

The fourth problem will be that you are too busy to invest time in developing talent in your organisation, instead hoping that HR will take up the slack.

Next you will really start to piss people off and this will have an impact on their motivation and performance, thereby doing even more damage to the bottom line potential of your organisation.

There is of course a potentially deeper chasm, both for you and for the business. What if you remain stuck at Level 2 and yet you have managed to successfully navigate your way to a leadership position, surviving all of the associated stress, burn-out and people's frustration with you, without ever having made the transition from high Performer to Manager? There are many, many people in senior leadership positions today who have accomplished this very piece of sorcery.

Think about this. You were already working flat out to try to cope as a bogus Manager, papering over the cracks in your team's performance and morale. The size of your new organisation has increased ten-fold. How long do you think you can survive now?

How long do you think that you can continue to kid people that you are valuable to the organisation? How much more damage needs to be done before it becomes catastrophic for the business and for your already badly damaged reputation?

BITE SEVEN

Restore Colour Balance at Work

Value the right blend of behavioural styles

Welcome back for our final exploration of the four colours. I have rightfully given extreme Reds a hard time, so I will now give the poor fellows (typically alpha males) a break.

At the end of Chapter 6, I briefly looked at blue, green and yellow Elephants. No colour is perfect for leadership on its own, but if I was forced to pick one it would be yellow, because of the pace, people orientation and influential qualities. In reality, a blend of colours is most effective, because one colour will have a modifying effect on the other and this balance can be very powerful.

The most powerful balance is when there is a strong orientation towards both people and results. A red/yellow or yellow/red blend is a very powerful one, especially in a faster-moving organisation, where more ambiguous and challenging decisions need to be made at speed. In a different kind of organisation, where quality and accuracy as well as execution are important, the green/blue or blue/green blend could be particularly effective.

There are roles where the red/blue blend or the green/yellow blend can thrive, but these blends are lacking in either the people side or the results/task side, so it requires wise thinking and honest conversations if you are considering putting such a person in a senior position.

A green/yellow blend could make a wonderful coach or counsellor and they will have excellent people skills. These are good qualities indeed, especially at a one to one level, but are they enough?

A blue/red blend could be quite good technically, or in projects, because they successfully manage the trade-off between their need for quality and their need to hit deadlines. This sounds great, but this type of person could struggle with relationships and their inner tension could spill over into their team.

There is one saving grace, however, and that is where their behavioural style is positively influenced by a third colour. This can make an immense difference to the hiring decision, because balance has been restored.

The historical tendency to favour task focus over people focus is a worry for me, to the extent that I believe it has fuelled a lot of the problems in leadership that are so prominent today. In the NHS, would we hear about such scandalous leadership behaviours, including bullying and intimidation, if their leaders had a stronger people focus? In Financial Services, would we have seen the same levels of greedy self-serving leadership? I wonder.

CHAPTER SEVEN – Summary and Final Thoughts

The main premise of this chapter was that there is an overarching behavioural style that must be understood, and then addressed, if we are to successfully understand, and then eat, the Elephant in the Room. Whilst sharing thoughts on providing self-help for red Elephants, we concluded that we must use our understanding of the risks involved in putting extreme Reds (leaders who are extremely fast paced and who demonstrate low people focus) in charge.

We must use this learning to inform the talent decisions that we make and the actions that we take with extreme Reds that are already in senior positions. If the treatment fails, it is a business imperative that they are removed. This is to secure the future good of the organisation.

We also explored the path to leadership across two chasms – a metaphor to describe the huge impact on reputation and bottom line results that occurs if we fail to get the right managers and leaders in place. We must be explicit and hold all managers and leaders accountable for making a successful transition into role, rewarding those who succeed and removing those who fail.

Finally, we concluded that whilst extreme red leadership equals extreme danger for the organisation, any other single extreme colour or behavioural style has leadership limitations. The most effective leadership style is the colour blend that demonstrates a strong focus on both results and people, irrespective of relative pace.

We have arrived at the end of our Main Course, but are far from finished with our dining strategy. Even the most extreme example of the Elephant in the Room must surely have a sweet tooth. Let's see if we can win him (or her) around in our Final Course.

How to Eat the Elephant in the Room

FINAL COURSE

Elephant TURNOVER

"The bottom line is the bottom line."

During the Main Course, we addressed two of our key words, Judging and Understanding. A massive ingredient of the DNA of the Elephant in the Room is our natural human tendency to judge each other and to do it in a way that is typically manifested in a subtle (or not-so-subtle) air of disapproval. I also told you that investing the time in understanding, first ourselves and then each other, puts us in pole position for success, at least in formulating our personal dining strategy.

Our final two key words are Appreciating and then Valuing. The gift of understanding enables us to develop a more finely-tuned ability to diagnose the kind of stuff that goes on at work and in life as part of natural, normal human behaviour. That heightened awareness firstly brings us to a place, practically a default position, where it is inevitable that we will start to appreciate each other a lot more.

That sense of appreciating, fuelled by our understanding, results in a different kind of perception that enables us to almost unconsciously look at each other differently than before. It enables us to develop different attitudinal lenses and change the filters that we may have unfairly put in place, with respect to the way in which we previously judged others. It is remarkable. These fresh, positively oriented filters lead us to a sense of valuing, to all intents and purposes a 'halo effect', where we can now see the potential and significant value of the very same people at whom we had previously been frowning negatively.

Nothing has changed except our understanding, but this understanding is the secret ingredient, the catalyst for a remarkable positive change in our outlook towards our fellow human beings. If this sounds like a worthwhile outcome, please read on!

The Final Course is called Elephant Turnover for a reason. I absolutely believe that the purpose of most companies is to grow, to be profitable and to make money. Whilst I'm passionate about coaching and the opportunity to develop managers, leaders and winning teams, my passion does not just come from my belief in the potential of people. Coaching works because of the profound benefits in terms of bottom line results. My passion used to get me into trouble, because I knew it worked and hounded people for not getting it!

Today I remain passionate and excited by this because leadership is under the spotlight like never before. I know that great coaching and great leadership deliver incredible bottom line results for leaders and their organisations. And that is why the Final Course is called Elephant Turnover.

I truly believe that one of the lynchpins of sustained growth and success for my company and any other company is the power of relationships.

Relationships are woefully neglected in many large companies and the further up the organisation you go, the worse it gets. As a leader, the time has come for you to stop using the excuse that you are 'too busy' to invest time in relationships. You know by now how I feel about this excuse. You will not like it – I'm relentless. Resistance is futile!

Chapter 8, Sweetly Glazed Elephant Waffle, is all about creating an atmosphere that is toxic for the Elephant in the Room. Things are going to get so positive, so affirmative and so deliciously 'sweet' that by the time we are finished with our metaphorical Elephant, it will have the glazed look of contentment of a beast that has just gone ten rounds of coaching with the Dalai Lama.

We will be examining the word Appreciating in Chapter 8, with a strong focus on the essence of what works in organisations. We will talk about containing the Elephant and I will share more useful bites of the Elephant. This will include a look at my philosophy about coaching and building a coaching culture. It will also include a strong recommendation for something called Appreciative Enquiry, which is incredibly powerful.

Chapter 9 is deliciously called Elephant Parfait, which brings a cool, powerful metaphor alongside our final key word, Valuing. We will continue to share more bites of the Elephant, in the form of story-telling, language, metaphor, empowerment and strengths. I will share with you my leadership principles of GIVE. In addition, I will give you a flavour of some of my other tools and best practices, including my MAX Potential model of career development and my Winning PERFormance System.

In terms of value, I remain excited by the potential that we can unleash together. Everything that I'm sharing with you really does work. If you take it on board and apply it, it will be very hard for you to fail, unless of course you are too busy to succeed.

How to Eat the Elephant in the Room

CHAPTER EIGHT

SWEETLY GLAZED Elephant WAFFLE

"When you have got an Elephant by the hind legs and it is trying to run away, it's best to let him run."

Abraham Lincoln

A person I know very well once sought to justify his behaviour by saying, "It's in my nature". He is a great guy, but he sometimes exhibits the most selfish and unacceptable behaviour. I can smile when I observe the behaviour, because I know the person and I know his behavioural profile, but I can also successfully challenge him and provide him with feedback, because I know what works.

The extreme red behavioural style is a case in point. As I mentioned in Chapter 7, it is an eye-catching style because of the hard driving, single minded focus that is exhibited, and one that gets richly rewarded, thus providing more oxygen and affirmation to a set of behaviours that are ultimately destructive in organisations.

When you read about extreme red behaviour at the start of Chapter 7, you may have reflected on some of the stories from earlier chapters and the kind of leadership behaviour that led to the scandals in the NHS, BBC, Financial Services and many other areas, including the last Labour Government that was led by a dreadful leader, an intolerant, self-serving bully. You may have asked "Why does this behaviour get so richly rewarded?".

BITE EIGHT

Contain the Elephant

Develop the herd

Let me present you with a scenario to reflect on, and one question: What would YOU do?

The scenario is this. Your company's senior leadership team is frequently described by colleagues as dysfunctional. In fact, some of the directors on the team laughingly describe it as dysfunctional too. Recent 360 degree data shows that the team scores highly on just one of a number of leadership attributes and that is for functional expertise. One director joked that they were not promoted to the team for their leadership skills, which were non-existent, but because they worked hard, knew their part of the business and didn't piss anybody off.

Leadership team meetings are chaotic, with team members reading and sending emails and talking to each other during presentations. The quality of decision making is at best patchy and decisions are frequently changed. All the team members work extremely long hours, including many weekends, and many of them frequently look stressed out and exhausted, but will never admit to this. Some directors get irritable for the smallest of reasons and will publicly berate more junior managers in their organisation. Employee engagement scores decline over a number of years. There is just one woman on the team, who is well respected and highly competent.

One common complaint from the CEO and in 360 degree feedback is that the team is too tactical and not strategic enough. At rare off-site meetings, when leadership development is discussed, there is strong buy-in to the proposed development strategies. Some of the directors will enthusiastically sign up as sponsors of various initiatives, after hearing the empirical evidence which proves that these initiatives will contribute a significant return on investment in terms of bottom line results and employee engagement.

Unfortunately, little materialises from these initiatives due to work pressures and conflicting priorities that emerge after the commitments were made. Occasionally, a director will react angrily if they are challenged about their failure to meet these commitments.

Over time, employee frustration grows. The same directors have been in place for many years, there is no obvious focus on succession planning and the general impression is that directors are protecting their own positions. As leadership capability grows stronger and stronger in the rest of the organisation, below the leadership team, mutterings at the coffee machine continue. The frustration eventually comes to a head in an off-site meeting, when a confidential question is aired through the electronic audience response system.

The response to the question "Does our leadership team walk the talk as leaders?" elicits a 75% NO response. At this point, the CEO looks to you and says "Shit! What are we going to do?".

Is this a scenario that strikes a chord for you? It represents a composite picture of my own experiences and that of many friends and contacts of mine who encountered similar conditions in many different companies. What would YOU do in such a situation?

When I look back at some of my own attempts to make a difference in factors pertaining to the Elephant in the Room, I reflect on things that I might have done better. A key learning point for me was this – think carefully before you confront the Elephant. If it feels cornered, it may react aggressively and make a lot of noise. In extreme cases one angry Elephant may trigger a stampede, in which case, you're in real trouble.

At least I have recognised in my own leadership work over the years that the definition of insanity is doing the same things again and again, hoping for a different result. Unwittingly, but fortunately, I found myself to be applying Stephen Covey's principles of Circle of Influence (versus his Circle of Control). Instead of reacting to things over which I had little control, I learned to put my energy into making a difference in areas in which my team and I could do something.

That doesn't mean that you should stop investing time and energy in trying to win hearts and minds at the top. Please continue to do that, but realise that whilst you can elicit good intentions and, on occasion, even some hard commitments, the realities of work pressures will kick in for the leaders who make those commitments.

Ultimately, despite wonderful intentions, even leaders at the top of the organisation may not feel empowered to sustain development as a priority over urgent short-term tactical issues, even though the rewards for doing so are far greater for the organisation. Now that's a form of insanity.

In one case, after realising where our true circle of influence was, my team and I developed a containing strategy. (Note: This is not the kind of thing that you advertise.) We became highly proficient at developing new managers, existing managers and middle managers. We saw this as our biggest opportunity to make a difference.

If the wrong people are in place at the top, then the greater opportunity is to ensure that you get the right people on the bus further down the leadership pipeline. After all this is a much more significant group of people, not only in size, but in the fact that one day, some of the people you are developing will be members of the top team.

By setting the right standards for manager performance and, over time, developing the right kind of managers who are capable of crossing chasms and who are more likely to develop into effective leaders, you are more likely to succeed. But it will take a long time.

For leaders in your organisation, if their reputation and potential value to the organisation are stuck in a deep chasm, you can throw them as many ropes as you want. Ultimately, it has to be their decision to climb out.

Another thing that I have learned, that has become part of the mission statement for my own company, is this: Respect the time constraints of my clients. We don't live in a perfect world and sometimes, we need to put our utopian ideas to one side in favour of optimistic pragmatism. We live in a world that hurtles along at internet speed. We have to acknowledge reality and sometimes work around it, rather than rail against it.

We have a choice. We can stand miserably on the side-lines and complain about our leaders, or we can try to help them as best we can. Yes, many of them are dysfunctional. Yes, many of them are unfit for purpose and should be taken as far away from positions of leadership as possible. Yes indeed, many of them are too busy to do the very things that will deliver far greater long-term results. And yes, many of them are stuck in a world of internet speed pain. But at least we can try to help them.

I learned a lot through failure as well as success. I learned to try to understand the Elephant rather than antagonise it. My own focus on developing the herd was largely successful. I wish I could have been more successful in turning around dysfunctional leaders, but as I said, it's ultimately more productive to understand and appreciate your circle of influence and win where you can.

We're all trying to make a difference as best we can, when time is a scarce commodity. You are no different and finding time to focus on your development is hard. But it's not impossible. We can all find at least the odd hour here and there; it's how we make the best use of limited time that absorbs me.

Somebody once asked me what would be my number one leadership priority. If I had limited budget and just one area that I could focus on, what would it be? Without a moment's hesitation, I replied using just one word – coaching.

It feels good to get positive feedback for your coaching skills, even if it is more of a comment on your positive attitude towards people, rather than a true skills assessment. It took many years for me to agree with any such views that had been expressed about my coaching capability.

Coaching is a potent combination of a number of key skills. In addition, I know that a skilled coach can leap over chasms with ease. In other words, a skilled coach will easily acquire other leadership skills as they apply their coaching expertise, under their own steam and without the need for much external assistance. This makes coaching strategically important.

BITE NINE

Develop a coaching culture in your company

Use it to Unlock Potential and Unleash Talent

The person who inspired me to become an evangelist on the subject of building a coaching culture is Carole Gaskell, who is Managing Director of Full Potential Group, which she founded in 1998. What I am sharing with you below is a modified version of what I learned from Carole. I therefore bow and pay homage to her genius. Before I met Carole Gaskell, I always used the words 'strategic imperative' to describe the importance of coaching to the leaders who I supported, in an effort to connect coaching to hard business results.

What is a Coaching Culture?

When an organisation concludes that coaching is directly connected to results and should be at the heart of management and leadership performance, it is heading towards building a coaching culture. When leaders decide to develop and embed coaching as the predominant management skill and the main basis for working together, they have started working on the strategy.

There are five simple building blocks that will lead to the development of a coaching culture:

1. Secure top-down buy-in and ownership

2. Develop a compelling strategy and plan

3. Provide learning solutions and integrated support

4. Measure and monitor success against key indicators

5. Ensure sustainability over time.

Ultimately, building a coaching culture is a business strategy, but it is not sufficient for the senior team to seek someone else in HR or a subordinate to take ownership for it because they are too busy with other work. Let's look at each of the five components in a little more detail.

Secure top-down buy-in and ownership

When presenting the case for coaching to the board, it is always a good idea to check who has received coaching in the past. They will probably be advocates and potential sponsors. Speak to each of them separately in order to sound them out about your proposal and to secure their support. They might also be interested in being active sponsors for the proposal, both in securing board approval and rolling out the initiative. They might even be interested in taking advantage of any available personal development benefits for themselves.

It is also important to provide as much empirical evidence as possible about the significant return on investment that can be achieved from coaching, along with some success stories or case studies from other companies.

Develop a compelling strategy and plan

Securing buy-in is an important step, but only a small part of the work that needs to be done in order to successfully build a coaching culture. A compelling vision of the desired end state must be clear, specific and commonly understood by all board members. In fact, it should be so clear and desirable that they can practically smell it!

Board members are busy people. Make it easy for them to support and sponsor the strategy.

Below is a simple diagram that I have used for many years in order to illustrate my proposed approach to developing the strategy.

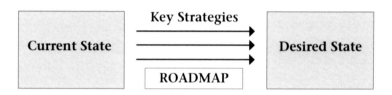

Think like a project manager when you articulate the strategy and outline the plan. Consider risks and call out potential barriers to success. Articulate a clear current state so that the desired state looks even more compelling. The benefits of doing this are solid. It's much easier to get a feel for the distance between the two and it is much easier to articulate the key strategies and specific measurable outcomes that will take you in the right direction and in realistic time frames.

Provide learning solutions and integrated support

Coaching training is great. I should know. I have received a lot and designed a lot myself. But, whilst you will get significant return on investment from providing a portfolio of learning solutions, you will not realise the cosmic return that building a coaching culture will give.

Again, thinking like a project manager will lead you to conclude that the following activities are important:

- Connect the overall strategy to existing talent and leadership development strategies

• Consider some kind of connection to compensation or reward systems that reflect the value of coaching

• Design a communications plan to promote the strategy and keep people informed about progress

• Embed a regular stakeholder review process so that all sponsors and key parties remain fully informed and engaged.

Measure and monitor success against key indicators

Many development initiatives get off to a great start and then wither on the vine as competing priorities win the day. If key success indicators have been agreed from the outset and a process has been put in place to track performance against these indicators, there is a greater chance of sustainable and long-term success. A simple dashboard can be created, which will maintain interest and commitment in the strategy. A few positive indicators can go a long way!

Ensure sustainability over time

In my experience, it is so easy to become cynical when an important initiative becomes superseded by a new, cooler HR idea. How do you ensure that coaching remains on the radar and that the leadership team don't forget that coaching is part of the DNA of leadership excellence?

Measuring and monitoring success is important. Equally important is to have a sub-strategy to grow the base of powerful advocates and coaching champions from the top down. Your key sponsors on the board may leave the company. Who will replace them as coaching advocates? The more organic you can make this the better. In other words, you will know you are winning when it is the sponsors and coaching champions who actively create sustainability by bringing more senior people into the coaching fold.

More than anything else, if you do it right, you will create a snowball effect because the more coaches you develop, the more obvious the benefits of coaching will become through improved results and leadership capability. A good coach becomes very passionate about the value of coaching to the business!

I am pleased to say that the coaching culture initiative that I left behind at Intel is continuing to flourish and when I had a conversation with Carole Gaskell, I reminded her about the inspiration that she had provided me with.

I also asked Carole a few Elephant-related questions.

Carole, what's your big Elephant in the Room?

"Culture is a big one, but one specific issue for me is emotional buy-in. A lot of leaders operate at an intellectual level and they may make rational assessments on the people side, but lack the emotional connection. A lot of leadership behaviour is not adult to adult and many leadership behaviours do not reflect a coaching approach. There are many small opportunities for leaders to be a coach and they need to seize these opportunities."

What distracts leaders from seizing these moments?

"It very much depends on the leader. If they are constantly in performance mode and their focus is on them and their impact as the expert, they are more likely to feel that they have to tell or advise people. They demonstrate an ingrained behaviour where they do a lot of talking and very little listening, or asking questions. It's a hard-wired behaviour."

Do you have any advice on how to eat the Elephant?

"You mentioned building trust and I agree with that. The other one for me is courage. People don't give each other honest feedback and if they could only find the courage to take a risk and do that, it could make a difference."

Carole's thoughts on courage triggered another C word for me and that word is Curiosity. Please reflect on this thought. If you truly believe in the potential of people, will you enable them to realise their full potential if it is YOU that does the work for them?

Your belief in the potential of others means that you will be very interested, in fact, most curious, about the ideas that will emerge during the coaching conversations that you have with them. Please allow that sense of curiosity to be your spirit guide during your leadership journey, and allow your curiosity to be the power behind the questions that you ask. You may be amazed at the powerful impact that they will have in terms of improved performance and improved trust.

APPRECIATING

During Chapter 5, we chewed over the three terrible triggers of quarkiness that have been with us for many decades and which will remain with us unless we address them. I talked to you about Silicon-Thinking and Deficit-Thinking, where we maintain a persistent level of intolerance about that which we find to be less than perfect. In fact, our attitudes have become so embedded that we will always find something to be dissatisfied about. Human DNA is imperfect – we will never be disappointed.

The above thinking, allied with a Theory X mentality that reflects our negative views about the desire and motivation of workers, is not good for business. I have my own theory that this negative view about people has led to huge levels of dependence in organisations, where employees and even managers are unable to function without direction. They are so dependent that they need to be told what to do – and frequently how to do it – before they can contribute.

So what is Theory Y?

The management thinking under Theory X believes that people are lazy and, in order to secure results, rewards need to be offered. The beliefs of Theory Y are that the real challenge for management is to create the culture and working environment where workers can develop and showcase their great potential.

I have found it highly amusing that some leaders believe that by offering free fruit and subsidised or free coffee and soft drinks they will improve engagement. What about changing the culture and showing more trust in people?

Do you remember the Robert Rosenthal rat story that I shared with you in Chapter 6? In 1964, Rosenthal also conducted an experiment in an elementary school in the USA to see whether or not teacher expectations influenced their students' performances. Teachers were told the names of children in their classes who were "late bloomers – about to dramatically spurt in their academic performance".

In fact, these 'gifted' children were randomly selected and were no smarter than their classmates. At the end of the academic period, the apparently gifted children not only performed better in the eyes of their teachers, but they also scored significantly higher on standardised IQ tests.

What if managers and leaders in organisations could imbue a similar 'halo effect' with respect to how their people were routinely perceived? What if all managers and leaders in organisations were encouraged to value the strengths of their people rather than seek out and destroy their weaknesses? Their potential for enhanced performance would be incredible.

BITE TEN

Think Affirmatively

Harness the Power of Appreciative Enquiry

The principles of Appreciative Enquiry are quite different to the deficit-thinking exhibited by defect-intolerant organisations that chips away at morale and sustainable performance. It is a form of thinking that seeks out the essence of what is great about an organisation, in order to magnify and widely disperse that essence of greatness throughout the organisation. I describe it as identifying the good stuff, bottling it, then sharing it and spreading the word.

Appreciative Enquiry was developed by Dr. David Cooperrider. It is a form of thinking and understanding that sees organisations as affirmative systems that are created by people as solutions to problems. Instead of seeking defects, errors and what is 'wrong' about an organisation, Appreciative Enquiry is an approach that seeks out what is 'right' about the organisation. In effect, it seeks to paint a series of compelling pictures that comprise the overall 'halo effect' of the organisation.

There are potentially remarkable outcomes just from participation in Appreciative Enquiry, because it seeks to identify what works, typically by gathering stories, thoughts, pictures and ideas from people based upon what they think, feel and do when they are at their best, at their peak.

In Chapter 6, I talked to you about self-awareness as a key component of emotional intelligence, which is at the heart of great leadership. Can you imagine the benefits of focusing uniquely on each one of us at our best and sharing that goodness with others? How do we feel when we're appreciated for who we are? How do we feel when we become more self-aware and value ourselves more? If we feel appreciated and we value ourselves more, what happens to our typically defensive reaction to change?

If we feel more valued, we become more open to learning, growth and future possibilities – the idea of what 'could be'. If we value ourselves more, we value others more as well. And guess what? They reciprocate! For each positive belief, there is an equal and opposite positive belief in return. As we luxuriate in the bath of positivity, we displace defect-seeking negativity.

BITE ELEVEN

Make Great Decisions

Harness the Power of Disagreement

My belief in the power of disagreement has become profound, but at its heart is some very early management development training that I delivered when I was at Intel.

One key component of the Intel culture, since the time of Andy Grove, was called 'constructive confrontation'. The idea was that in order to quickly solve problems and get things done, it was healthy to confront the issue, but never the person. In meetings, Intel also had a great philosophy of disagree and commit, which in management development work was packaged under the highly effective process of 'consultative decision-making'.

Before I describe the process, let me talk for a moment about meetings. In many organisations, we have completely lost the plot when it comes to the effective use of time spent in meetings. The abuse of time amounts to a productivity impact of at least 20%, which means that for an organisation of one thousand people, the equivalent of at least two hundred of them are spent sitting unhappily in meetings which add no value and are a complete waste of their time.

The purpose of meetings is primarily to bring people together in order to move the business forward, to get things done, to solve problems, to make decisions. I just want to focus on the decision-making part of meetings here.

Consultative Decision-Making

I have used consultative decision-making for years as a key component of my meetings and decision-making. The basic tenets of consultative decision-making are:

- A decision needs to be made and it is the leader who makes the decision; no voting or consensus is desired or encouraged.

- Everybody's contribution is required and all team members must be given the opportunity to contribute. In other words they 'take responsibility to teach' the decision-maker. Each team member is therefore consulted.

- Because team members have different opinions and different knowledge and experience that may be of importance to the issue in hand, they are empowered to disagree. This is critical to successful decision-making.

- The leader's responsibility is to learn from each team member in order to make the best decision. There may be little time available to make the decision, so each person may only have a short opportunity to contribute.

- The leader, as decision-maker, does not have to side with the majority, but they should quickly explain the rationale behind their decision at the end in order to secure the commitment of those team members who expressed an alternative opinion.

- When the leader makes their decision, the principle of disagree and commit kicks in. In other words, whilst team members are entitled to continue to disagree, they must support the decision. Their voice has been heard and there should be no emotion attached to their disagreement.

When I took responsibility for new teams, I used early team meetings as an opportunity to 'teach' my new team not only my ideas and values, but also how I operated as their manager. When I briefed them on how my team meetings worked, I described the 'power of disagreement' as a vital life-force within the team that would enable us to function well as a team and which helped me to make the best decisions on behalf of the team.

When I was L&D Manager at Intel, there was a junior member of my team based in Munich. She was clearly green (slower paced, people-focused) and quite introverted. Very quiet and respectful in meetings, she came across as almost timid. She was a caring, supportive team member and the thought of having to challenge a colleague would have been very stressful for her. I patiently encouraged her to try out some disagreement and see if she liked it!

One day, we were having a planning meeting and I outlined the purpose of the session, inviting ideas from the team. Suddenly I noticed her take a deep breath, then stand up, grab a marker and take control of the flip-chart. She had some ideas that she was determined to share and started talking. She had obviously been thinking about this moment for a while. A misguided colleague from the USA, who I had invited to the meeting, tried to interrupt her. He was sitting next to me. I immediately grabbed his arm in a vice-like grip and whispered into his ear, "Shut up, this is amazing!"

It took just a moment of courage on her part, but from that moment onwards, it felt as if she had been liberated. That sense of permission to disagree and the supportive reaction from the rest of the team helped her to find her voice in the team. She was still the same delightful, modest person, but she was empowered to disagree and it felt great. The more she disagreed with me, within reason, and the more she said no to me when I made a silly request, the prouder I felt.

CHAPTER EIGHT – Summary and Final Thoughts

This chapter covered a lot of important work. The purpose of sharing the idea of a 'containment strategy' with you was to encourage you not to give up when faced with inflexibility at the top. You just have to look for a different part of the Elephant in the Room to bite!

An increasing number of companies appreciate the value of coaching. If the important strategic proposition of building a coaching culture resonated with you and perhaps gave you some food for thought, please consider how you could leverage coaching in your business. Think about what you could do to either develop as a coach, or to embed coaching in your organisation. I promise you that you will not be disappointed if you make that choice.

As a coach, I am sustained by strong Theory Y beliefs about the unlimited potential of my clients. Appreciative Enquiry is another belief system that is driven by a powerful focus on what works in organisations. It is a relatively new area of opportunity and one that excites me greatly. Once again, you will not be disappointed if you make the decision to investigate how you might use it.

I closed by talking about decision-making, as a showcase for the exploration of the power of disagreement. By creating the right kind of environment where each person appreciates the vital role that they play in helping you, as a leader, to make the best possible decisions, we build not only a platform for sustainable success, but for highly engaged, high-performing teams.

Having said that Chapter 8 contained a lot of important work, guess what? I'm about to say the same about Chapter 9, where, as I promised, the underlying theme is Valuing, our final key word.

CHAPTER NINE

Elephant PARFAIT

"When an Elephant is in trouble, even a frog will kick him."

Hindu Proverb

I hate to see money being wasted or huge costs being unnecessarily incurred by organisations. This opportunity cost occurs when you either miss or ignore an opportunity that would have delivered a better return on investment to your business. It is the cost of NOT doing something that you should have done.

VALUING

People are our biggest asset. As our attitudes transform from 'judging' each other negatively to appreciating the potential that we each offer, despite all of our differences, then great things are possible. There is so much empirical evidence about the positive impact on the bottom line from the behaviours that people demonstrate towards each other that this has now become a hard business fact. The bottom line is that we add significant Value to the bottom line by putting the right people, with the right people behaviours, into leadership positions, and removing, or if possible rehabilitating, the wrong people.

In this chapter, I will provide you with more useful resources and a lot of valuable food for thought. This stuff works and you are empowered to select what works best for you. If you try it out, you will not be disappointed. It will provide real value for you and your organisation.

BITE TWELVE

Make Leadership a Competitive Advantage

Develop Leaders who GIVE

We can continue to complain, rightfully so, about the poor quality of leaders in our organisations, because I am not optimistic that much has changed in the last six years since the credit crunch and resultant recessions. However, if we are to avoid the insanity of making the same mistakes again and again by reverting to the same self-serving leadership styles, organisational cultures and contempt for employees and customers as before, then something needs to change.

I fear that there is little appetite for change. I fear that a sense of denial and defiance persists in many boardrooms. I fear that many leaders will continue to obsess about their personal needs and what they can take versus what they can give.

My principles of **GIVE** as a framework for effective leadership have been inspired by people like Noel Tichy and his 'Teachable Point of View' as well as Ken Blanchard and his 'Leadership Point of View'.

My principles of **GIVE** are also at the heart of my company name, igiveu. We have enough self-serving leaders who take. If only they knew that the more we give to others, the more we will receive in return.

GIVE is a simple acronym: Goals, Ideas, Values, Energy.

GOALS

If you are lousy at writing goals, you are a liability to your organisation. Do not pass Goal until you have developed this as a skill. It is a simple yet tremendous skill that will never let you down. In fact, mastery of goal-writing will put you further along the right track towards being more effective as a leader.

Great leaders write great goals. Many leaders work hard, but they do not necessarily work smart, and as a result they struggle to articulate their immense effort in terms of clear, simple, achievable objectives that are easily understood by their team members. Writing great goals is a skill, which, once mastered, will enable you as a leader not only to write great strategic objectives, but to understand the relationship between those objectives, their supporting goals and the resources required to achieve them. A great plan is simply a small number of great goals, written in order of relative priority, with some clarity and intelligence about the resources that each goal requires in order to be met.

Leaders who write great goals and create great plans are able to quickly generate a performance status against each goal, thus minimising time wasted on describing the work that has been done and instead optimising time spent on issue identification and resolution. This requires all of their team's participation and leads to truly interdependent group work.

IDEAS

If you are truly strategic as a leader, you will think beyond the short-term goals that you are now so skilful at articulating. If you are thinking about the future of your company and the part of the company that is under your leadership, then spend some time writing down your personal ideas on how that future can be even better. Your ideas should cover a variety of areas, from your strategic concepts about where and how the organisation will evolve in the coming years (your vision of the future) to your creative approaches to growing the business in the shorter term.

If you don't think you do this well, start now. By writing your ideas down, you are growing as a leader.

VALUES

Your values underpin those of the company, but they go further. The standards that you set and expect from others are what make you tick as a leader – from your sense of integrity as a leader and as a human being just like everyone else to your beliefs about how colleagues should be treated. Great leaders develop other great leaders, because they realise the strategic importance of doing so for the future of their organisations. Great leaders articulate their values explicitly. They shape their values to support the business.

Your values guide your organisation in the behaviour required to be a member of your organisation. In other words, if, like me, you share a desire to 'get the right people on the bus', then invest the time in articulating this as part of your values and teaching it to your team. Make it clear what you expect and don't expect in terms of how people work with each other and behave towards each other. It is perfectly legitimate to describe the kind of behaviours that you will not tolerate, such as bullying.

ENERGY

Great leaders not only emit energy though their own sense of commitment and passion, but they generate energy through the way in which they consistently communicate their ideas and values to others.

This does not happen by accident. Great leaders reflect deeply on how they can convey their own passion and energy to others in a way that inspires and energises them. Whether it is a chance meeting by the coffee machine, a regular one to one coaching conversation, a planned meeting, or a presentation to a large audience, a great leader will use each opportunity to energise others through their effective communication of their ideas and values.

Think about all the great leaders you have observed. They typically use anecdotes and stories to frame their own experiences, values and ideas. Think about how they inspired and energized you and how you would like to accomplish the same thing.

How do I GIVE?

By Thinking

Time is scarce for all of us, especially for those of us who are 'too busy'. However busy we are, all of us have short periods of time that we can use productively. Use these spare moments to reflect on your Ideas and Values. Write them down. It will only take a few minutes and it will define who you are as a leader.

By Communicating

Think about the different ways and the different places in which you interact with others in your role as a leader. If your objective is to energize people that you interact with in a way that is consistent with your ideas and values, it creates a virtuous cycle that will also positively affect your ideas and values. The stories that you tell as a leader will provide the frame for teaching your compelling ideas and values to others.

By Listening

A great leader not only teaches others about their ideas and values;

they also learn from others by listening to them carefully, with interest, respect and curiosity. People love to be heard. People love to feel that their feedback counts. All of this is energising.

What are the Benefits?

Your reputation: The very process of GIVE makes people better leaders. All of those moments that you invest in thinking about who you are as a leader and how you can improve makes you a better leader. Over time and step by step, your ideas and values mature. As you refine them and they become more broadly known, this is when your reputation is established.

As leaders step back from the day-to-day pressures of business and reflect on what they know, and indeed, what they don't know (but need to find out), they come to understand and appreciate their underlying assumptions about themselves as leaders, their organisation and business in general. When you recognise those assumptions, you can challenge yourself to question, refine and hone them in a positive manner, which benefits both your reputation and the organisation. When implicit knowledge becomes explicit, it can then be questioned, refined and honed, which benefits both the leaders and the organisation.

Consistency of message: If you are consistent in your message and how you express your ideas and values to others, you are truly a teacher. By ensuring that the same set of messages gets transmitted throughout your organisation, you maintain common alignment and a sense of purpose, with consistent values. You will also positively impact the speed of learning and change in your organisation, which leads us to the third benefit.

Great leaders develop other great leaders: We have talked about your important role as a teacher to your organisation. Through this, the very act of communicating your ideas and values enables you to achieve one of your most challenging yet most important tasks as a leader, and that is your responsibility for developing people. Many leaders try to develop other leaders by example, which is not so good if you are a commanding or pace-setting leader. It can also take a long time and leaves many of your important insights unspoken.

GIVE is an exercise in increasing your self-awareness and improving the potency of your communication. Over time, it will give you an explicit body of knowledge to debate, modify and pass on to others.

Please go back and have a look at The Two Chasms in Chapter 7 and ask yourself this question: If I can work out how to invest in small periods of time in my busy schedule to figure out what GIVE means to me as a leader, will it enable me to cross chasms and increase my value to the organisation? I know the answer to this question. Do you?

BITE THIRTEEN

Set Your People up for Success

Develop Winning PERFormance

I remember the old days in HR when the latest slogans were bandied about. My favourite one was 'Organisational Capability'. This was a beautiful term, which was meant to be all about the capacity of an organisation to accomplish its stated strategic objectives.

The problem was that the slogan was laden with presuppositions about the capacity of the HR organisation to not only rise above its daily grind to understand the strategic objectives, but to then figure out what an effective organisation, with the appropriate capacity, looked like. It assumed that the leaders in the organisation had the ability to step up from competing with each other to be strategic; it also presupposed they were able to work with HR to create the right organisation to support whatever strategic objectives that they had come up with. Given that so many leaders are 'too busy' to do this, it was no wonder that I was not the only one to be sceptical about the latest slogans. My big issue was all about the incapacity of the HR department or the business to actualise the slogan – to make it happen.

I have spent a lot of time thinking about how to do this and what follows is a distillation of part of that thinking. It is a piece of work that I do with managers and their teams and, whilst it focuses on individual tasks, it is much more than this. If a leader sets out to ensure that every member of their organisation is in a Winning

PERFormance system, then they will achieve a significant return on that investment of their time.

Many people in organisations around the world work hard, but without much of an idea about why they are doing the work, or how well they are doing it. I wonder how that makes them feel and what that means in terms of missed opportunity for their employers. If we could provide all employees with an incredibly simple means of improving their effectiveness, what a difference that could make for them and for the organisation!

What is Winning PERFormance?

There are just four simple components or questions to ask:

1. **Purpose:** Is each employee clear how each of the tasks that they perform as part of their job contributes to the greater goals of the team and wider organisation?

2. **Expectations:** For each part of their job, are they clear about what is expected from them in terms of quantity (how much), quality (how good) and time (when)? Is the output from each task summarised by a SMART goal?

3. **Resources:** Do they have access to all the tools, systems, processes and managerial support that they need in order to be successful?

4. **Feedback:** Are they able to track and measure their own performance against these expectations?

How do you know that each team member demonstrates Winning PERFormance potential? This is very simple – the answer must be YES to all four questions. If the answer is no to any one of these questions, they are not set up for Winning PERFormance. The good news is that you will know exactly what to focus on and what needs to be done to secure a YES.

How do you create Winning PERFormance?

It is a very straightforward process and it is also the kind of management work that is chasm-crossing.

1. Invest a day with your team in order to conduct a Winning PERFormance Audit.

2. Ask each team member to list out their key job tasks. Typically, a team member's job should be split into 3-7 key job tasks.

3. Ask team members to complete an audit sheet where they answer the above four questions for each of their tasks.

4. For each one, identify what each team member needs in order to answer YES to all four questions.

5. Ensure that, task by task, all of their needs are met.

The return on your investment in carrying out this exercise will be significant.

My work on Winning PERFormance was inspired by a person who has also been a great personal inspiration to me over the years. His name is Bill Daniels and I have known him for many years, from when he first certified me as a trainer on one of his management development programs. Bill truly understands what makes high-tech companies tick. This in-depth knowledge, combined with a skill in inventing games, enabled him to create many business simulations. The first one that I got the chance to try was called 'Breakthrough Systems', an amazing development activity using strips of paper, tape and marker pens. It sounds simple but it was simply amazing and an incredible aid to learning.

I was keen to ask Bill a few questions about Elephants.

Bill, what's your number one Elephant in the Room?

"In a word, me! In fact, the Elephant in the Room is all of us. We're getting in our own way all of the time. It's been like that for decades and it's all to do with the ego of the CEO, the board and their managers. We think it's all about us, but the real truth that is not being acknowledged is that management and leadership is NEVER about us. This cult of personality that we are seeing is a terrible distraction to the true work of the organisation. It's lurked there for years."

Where should managers and leaders focus their attention?

"The manager is there to serve all their individual contributors and give them what they need so that they can deliver on their commitments. They are there to ensure that customers are well served. Management is not about managers. It's how they empower their people and focus on their desired outputs, along with the people who deliver them."

What would be your first bite of the Elephant?

"We need to get managers focused on something more tangible – outputs. Clarity of outputs drives greater clarity of focus. If you focus on measurable outputs, you focus on the whole system and what your customers want. You create a feedback loop by ensuring that you have delivered enough outputs, on time; and based on what your customers think, you know that they are good enough. If there are problems, that's the job of the individual contributor to fix, not the leader. The leader should be asking, 'What resources can I provide?'"

You mentioned a cult of personality which I agree is a huge issue. What does a great leader look like to you?

"It's not about the elitist leadership culture which consists of egotistical leaders being fawned upon by their hired team of ego-strokers! It's about what people say about them while their egos are being massaged by some top dollar trainers at five star resorts.

I agree with Jim Collins, author of Good to Great, who says that it's essentially about being a servant leader. The best leaders find it difficult to talk about themselves because they are such great listeners and prefer to spend their time doing that. They are not egotistical and tend not to stand out very much in their organisation – they know it's not about them. They are trustworthy and demonstrate great integrity. They are deeply concerned about how the organisation delivers its desired outputs and pleases its customers and tend to be more distracted by how they can help their people accomplish this."

Why do people never learn from their poor choice of leadership?

"This is down to the unenlightened board of directors. They tend to be impatient and short-term in their thinking and do not allow great leaders the time that they need to build an organisation that is capable of sustainable results in the long term. They create a cycle of destruction, because their obsession with short-term results and tendency to put people in charge who they think will accomplish that, actually jeopardises the future of the company."

Do you have any feedback on my Winning PERFormance model?

"I like it very much. The content is fresh and very much in-demand. My big concern is that people are still not paying enough attention to this important area. I would strongly emphasise the importance of having clarity of Expectations. With regards to Feedback, we must ensure that our people have the ability to monitor performance while they're doing the work."

BITE FOURTEEN

Help Your People to Develop Their Career

Invest in MAX Potential

One of the most profound things that I have ever heard in respect to management development was from a piece of research which concluded that employees who had "regular, meaningful career development conversations" with their boss out-performed other employees, who did not have these conversations, by an average of 25%.

This was a simple and compelling piece of data which made so much sense to me as a coach, as the return on investment is so significant. Most managers and leaders would give their right arm for a performance improvement like that. It's such a shame that they are 'too busy' to do it, because few employees I have ever met have had such conversations with their boss. It was a simple nugget of data but it had quite a tremendous influence on me, inspiring my work in career development and career coaching over the years. This has culminated in my model of MAX Potential which I would now like to share with you.

There are three components of **MAX** Potential – Motivation, Abilities, eXperience – and one underlying assumption, that the organisation sees value in them.

Motivation

Do your employees enjoy the kind of work they are doing? Do they like the people they are working with? Do they have a good relationship with their boss? Do they feel confident? Do they demonstrate the right kind of attitude towards others? How they feel, how motivated they are and the strength of their commitment to the job will have a significant effect on their performance.

Abilities

Are you competent? Are you qualified? Do you meet the academic requirements for the role? Do you have the right skills to perform your job to the best of your ability? Does your boss agree? Do your colleagues agree? All of this is even more important if you are in a managerial or leadership position. We sometimes hope that hard work alone will compensate for gaps in our ability. Sometimes this works, but is it sustainable?

eXperience

How long have you been doing this job, or similar jobs? Have you had the opportunity to become an expert in your role? Have you had the time to learn from your mistakes? Are you still a learner? We sometimes use the old saying: "There's no substitute for experience". We may have some excellent transferable skills and qualifications, but it can take time to figure out how to apply these skills and be effective in our roles. If you lack motivation and you fail to do something about it, even if it is due to extrinsic factors, such as your boss, think carefully about the impact on your performance. Think even more carefully about what this will do to your MAX Potential.

AX Potential...

As a manager or leader, you can make a huge difference to the potential of all of your people. It is the responsibility of your people to perform, but you can be the catalyst for success, or failure, which might be AX Potential for you!

For each of your people, put in place regular meaningful career development conversations. In fact, go one step further and ensure that each team member has a development contract in place.

The Development Contract

Premise

It is the job of each employee to take full responsibility for owning their development and managing the process, over time, in partnership with their manager. They own it; their manager supports it. The organisation, in partnership with HR, provides the necessary resources, both internally and externally.

Issue

For some reason, many employees, managers and leaders invest a paltry amount of time in planning and managing their own development. They seem to think that it is the job of HR, or their boss, or somebody else, to develop them. They may even think that selecting a few days of training every year from a menu will have a miraculous effect where, through osmosis, they will acquire the necessary skills.

Opportunity

A recognised key principle of the Coaching profession is 'No Contract – No Coaching'. In other words, unless we agree on the focus and objectives of our work, with clearly defined outcomes that define what success will look like as a result of our work, there is no context or purpose; therefore no productive coaching can occur.

Exactly the same contracting principle applies to our future career development. By this I mean our future progress from a new hire, to a high-performing contributor, to a successful manager, to a future leader in the organisation. The development contract is therefore not just about our current job.

So, as part of the one to one discussions between employee and boss, it is critical that a specific development agenda is agreed. This should help the employee to first share their future aspirations within the company and then agree on a development path that will help them to get there successfully.

Part of the contracting process is agreeing what the words 'regular' and 'meaningful' mean. The rest of the contracting process is all about the what, the why and the how in our development. The contracting process is initiated by the employee and agreed, amended and supported by their manager.

Development is not training! It is a combination of training, coaching, on the job learning and a lot more besides, including mentoring, work assignments and projects.

The flip-side of the development contract of course is that in order to secure the support of their manager, the employee needs to use their new skills, knowledge and experience to deliver on their contracted performance expectations! This is how the company achieves ROI from investing in development.

BITE FIFTEEN

Grow Your Power by Sharing it with Others

Bake Power Pie

I promised that I would talk about Power Pie. This is not a big bite of Elephant, but it's an important one. A huge problem for both managers and leaders is 'letting go'. We have already established that and discussed it at great length in Chapter 7, while we navigated our way across The Two Chasms of leadership.

A principle that is core to my leadership beliefs and one that we covered when we talked about Leaders who GIVE is the principle that 'Great leaders develop other great leaders.' How will you ever achieve this if you are unable, unwilling, or just 'too busy' to let go of work that other people in your organisation can complete just as easily as you can?

My heroes all agree. Ken Blanchard talks about developing self-reliant achievers in organisations and yes, at some early point they required direction from you as you guided them on their journey to greatness, but not anymore.

Marshall Goldsmith talks about giving power to those who have demonstrated the capacity to handle the responsibility. Marshall also talks about creating a favourable environment in which people are encouraged to grow their skills and giving people discretion and autonomy over their tasks and resources.

On the other hand, Daniel Goleman talks about the damage that is done to organisations by firstly the pace-setting (do what I do) leadership style and secondly the commanding (do what I say) leadership style. There are serious pie-related issues here.

So, if power is your thing, the way to grow it is to give it away! I do realise that if you are a psychopath you will use your charm to make people believe that they are empowered, but we know that they are not. They are merely stepping stones to your personal ambitions. If you are an extreme Red, or one of Daniel Goleman's commanding or pace-setting leaders, you will tell people that they are empowered and then tell them what to do and how to do it; and by the way it's urgent.

Just draw a picture of a pie and imagine creating a lot of small slices in that pie, which you freely share with others. Now imagine what happens to that small slice of your Power Pie. It grows. In a year's time, imagine what has happened to all of the small slices of your Power Pie that you gave away. They have all grown substantially.

Now extrapolate your vision of pie from one year to five years. Your Power Pie is no longer the individual pie that you held closely to your chest and were too suspicious of the agendas, abilities and motivations of others to share it with them. That pie only grew slightly, if at all.

How big do you think that small puny individual pie of yours might be in five years' time compared to your shared pie? The difference will be pretty astonishing. So what's stopping you slicing your Power Pie right now? After all, all it requires is 'letting go'...

BITE SIXTEEN

Don't Just Settle for Being a Good Leader

Be Extraordinary

In everything we do, we all have a choice. If you are already in a senior leadership position and you are reading this, you may have been reflecting on how you are perceived as a leader by the rest of the people in your organisation. What kind of things are they saying about you at the coffee machine that you will never hear them say to you directly?

Early in Chapter 2, I mentioned the leadership research conducted by another one of my heroes, Jack Zenger, and his partner Joe Folkman. I promised you that I would share some thoughts that Jack shared with me during a conversation that we had in November 2013. Jack was one of the leadership development thought leaders that I had looked up to for many years. He was up there with people like Marshall Goldsmith, Ram Charan and others, including my good friend Bill Daniels.

I had previously spoken to Jack in 2006, a few years after he and Joe Folkman had completed their research and created their excellent 'Extraordinary Leader' program. I was keen to hear about how the program was going and get a few thoughts from Jack about the unspoken truth in organisations.

Here's how he replied to my questions.

What does 'Elephant in the Room' mean to you?

"When there are a lot of areas that are off-limits for discussion, you know there's a problem. Everybody knows it, yet nobody dares to talk about it. It's politically incorrect. Nobody wants to cross a senior person with great power. They dance around. It's UNSPEAKABLE!"

What kind of things do you believe feed the Elephant?

"It depends on the organisation, because some are worse than others. If there's a high power distance, with a huge separation between leaders at the top and people at lower levels of the organisation, that could be a contributor. If there is a dominant figure at the top in the organisation who is revered but also feared, because they are authoritarian and have a record of punishing people who have spoken up in the past, then that's an even bigger problem. It has a lot to do with the culture, which may have grown around the leadership of just one person."

In Chapter 2 of this book, I talked about Expertise. One of your five pillars of Extraordinary Leadership is Personal Capability. I do worry that decision makers set too great a store on expertise when they make decisions about leadership potential. What's your view?

"In our research, technical expertise is highly correlated with perceived success but if it stands alone, that's not enough. Technical expertise is important, but it becomes an issue if it's the only thing and not balanced with any other skill, or other strengths. The other strengths don't have to be great, but they cannot be awful and where we see leaders with high technical expertise and awful relationship skills, or strategic skills, they will never be a good leader."

If there was just one thing (apart from the Extraordinary Leader program) that you would recommend to my readers about how to eat the Elephant in the Room, what would it be?

"If I was only allowed one recommendation it would have to be Coaching. One of my colleagues (Kathleen Stinnett) is a Master Certified Coach and that inspired me to work with her in co-authoring a book called 'The Extraordinary Coach'. Coaching puts into operation most of the research about what makes effective leaders. It is also strongly connected to 'inspires and motivates', one of our extraordinary leader behaviours that is most correlated to higher levels of engagement and performance."

The 5 Pillars of Extraordinary Leadership

It was wonderful to catch up with Jack again. Not only was I thrilled that he agreed with me on coaching as the number one recommendation for those who wish to develop a dining strategy to eat Elephants, but he gave me a new word to play with: unspeakable!

The unspeakable behaviour that makes people afraid to speak up and which contributes to a culture that is toxic to engagement and performance does not exist within the realms of Extraordinary Leadership. Here are a few brief nuggets to summarise the research that underpins the program.

There are 5 Pillars of Extraordinary Leadership:

1. Character

2. Personal Capability

3. Focus on Results

4. Interpersonal Skills

5. Leading Change

The research conducted by Jack Zenger and Joe Folkman showed that top performing leaders might only have two or three of the above pillars as core strengths. However, by investing time in developing these into outstanding strengths, whilst avoiding any major derailers or weaknesses (fatal flaws), their resultant leadership effectiveness and value to the organisation became significant.

In Chapter 7, I shared some simple relative indicators of value to the organisation in The Two Chasms, where the ability to successfully 'let go' of the and work in order to make the tough transition to manager and leader delivered a relative centile value of 60% and 90%.

The Zenger-Folkman research shows something similar:

- If they demonstrate no outstanding strengths and no major weaknesses, a leader's effectiveness is just 34%.

- If they successfully build one of the five pillars as a top quartile strength, their effectiveness leaps to 64%.

- If they exhibit just two top quartile strengths, their effectiveness increases to 74%.

Their research implies that the time that you spend developing yourself will be best spent in areas where you are already strong.

This also correlates with the research conducted by Marcus Buckingham, the Gallup Organisation and others about the positive impact and benefits of playing to people's strengths. I know that Marcus Buckingham, another one of the greatest researchers and thought leaders of our time in this area, believes that companies who invest in cultivating their employees' strengths, rather than demonstrating the usual tendency to simply fix their weaknesses, will achieve dramatically improved efficiency and results, as well as personal growth, engagement and success from the recipients.

CHAPTER 9 – Summary and Final Thoughts

I'm still enjoying the word 'unspeakable' from my conversation with Jack Zenger. It says so much about the subject matter of this book and many of the leadership behaviours that we have explored together.

The concept of GIVE is one that very important to me and reflects many of my own values and beliefs. If you invest just small amounts of time in reflecting on your own leadership approach and how you could be an even better leader, using GIVE as your guide, you will not be disappointed in the outcome.

I have successfully used Winning PERFormance with clients. Imagine what the impact could be if every single member of your team, with your help, was in full control of their job and the outputs from the work that they do. If you find that the kind of career development conversations that you have with your people are enhanced by the MAX Potential model, you may very well see a positive shift in their engagement and results.

As you reel from the shock of these incredible changes for the better, you may be tempted to create your own Power Pie and share it with members of your organisation. You know that your power will increase beyond what you had previously thought possible, but it will be a different kind of power. It will be an extraordinary power, because you realise what an Extraordinary Leader you could become by simply discovering and developing your core strengths as a leader and ensuring that there are no fatal flaws in your leadership.

Thus ends our Final Course, Elephant Turnover. I wouldn't get up and go to the bar just yet, because no good dinner is complete without an After Dinner Speech.

AFTER DINNER SPEECH

What time is it when an Elephant sits on your fence?

It's time to build a new fence.

In 1976, Peter Finch, the great British actor, played the role of aging TV news anchor Howard Beale in the wonderful movie 'Network'. The following extract from a Howard Beale speech towards the end of the film nicely captures the essence of one of the more visceral elements of my dining strategy.

"I don't have to tell you things are bad. Everybody knows things are bad. It's a depression. Everybody's out of work or scared of losing their job. The dollar buys a nickel's worth, banks are going bust... I don't know what to do about the depression and the inflation and the Russians and the crime in the street. All I know is first you've got to get mad. You've got to say, "I'm a Human Being goddammit, my life has value!"

So I want you to get up now. I want you all to get up out of your chairs. I want you to get up right now and go to the window, open it and stick your head out and yell, "I'm as mad as hell and I'm not going to take this anymore!""

The film was nominated for an Oscar but lost out to 'Rocky' with Sylvester Stallone – no doubt due to the testosterone-driven decision-makers who called the shots at the time. The film was released 38 years ago – it could have been yesterday.

So my question to you is this: How mad do you need to get before you will decide that you are not going to take this anymore? I said earlier in this book that the definition of insanity is 'doing the same thing again and again, hoping for a different result'. Would you put somebody who is insane in charge of a large organisation?

In this moment of madness, I have been briefly reflecting about the overall level of insanity of the Elephant in the Room, so please indulge me while I explore the following even more extreme thought. There is some speculation about the number of psychopaths who are in senior leadership positions today. It is estimated the number of people in our general population who have psychopathic tendencies is 1% and this is reckoned to rise to between 3% and 4% in senior leadership positions. I agree with that estimate.

Psychopaths may display egocentric, self-serving behaviour and will completely lack empathy or conscience. They may be charismatic, charming and adept at manipulating people in one-on-one interactions. They will flourish in large businesses, because their advancement can be influenced by their ability to favourably impress the boss. Psychopathic qualities of charm, charisma and grandiosity may be mistaken for vision, confidence, character and the 'assertiveness' that is so valued in leaders.

I believe that it only takes a small number of intolerant, bullying, or psychopathic leaders to pollute the leadership pipeline of an organisation, or to drive the wrong kind of culture. They create the kind of culture that favours only them and which is toxic to normal decent human beings. I have heard the word 'toxic' used many, many times by people in the past few years to describe the leadership of their organisation.

Even in the workshop that I recently attended with Daniel Goleman, the word 'toxic' was used several times in such a way by a number of disillusioned participants. When I hear that word, it is usually followed by the word 'dysfunctional'. So, what are we going to do about it? Well, let me tell you one thing we're going to do right now. I want you to get up right now and go to the window of your office, open it and stick your head out and yell:

"I'm as mad as hell and I'm not going to take this anymore!"

How to Eat the Elephant in the Room

CHAPTER TEN

THE BABY Elephant IN THE ROOM

"Sometimes I wonder whether the world is being run by smart people who are putting us on or by imbeciles who really mean it."

Mark Twain

I mentioned women in Chapter 2, where I briefly talked about the 2006 Talent conference in Dublin that I had attended as a speaker. During my presentation, I had caught the eye of one of the conference sponsors, Catalyst, when I spoke up for women in leadership. Their President, Ilene Leng, invited me to attend a meeting with her team, where they shared the findings from their recent report.

Their report identified gender stereotyping as the primary root cause for the continued lack of women in executive leadership positions. In other words, men truly believe, despite empirical evidence to the contrary, that they make better leaders than women.

Many millions of dollars have been invested in diversity initiatives over the past few decades, including gender diversity. Whilst we have made some progress on race, I feel that we have made minimal progress on gender. It is a very complicated issue and one which I feel has not had sufficient support from male leaders in organisations. When I come across more enlightened male leaders, such as Robert Baker, who share beliefs similar to mine about the importance of women in senior leadership positions, it gives me a real boost.

During the panel discussion at the Talent conference, I had a lively debate with the other male panellist, who had described most of the senior women that he had worked with as 'real bitches'.

I remember hesitating before coming back at him, because he had a point; I too had experienced the same thing. In my last corporate job, I remember with disappointment having to work with some extreme red, aggressive, self-serving and ruthlessly ambitious females. Sadly, some of them were HR Directors – the very people who are supposed to be supporting the development of talent in the organisation.

Where we differed was that I would gladly tolerate that sense of disappointment if it took us further towards parity, because our experiences were a symptom of the prevailing culture. Whilst it's a shame, I don't blame women for playing the alpha male game in order to get on. We just need the right women.

BITE SEVENTEEN

Men must let Women get on Top!

Build the strategic case for more women on the board

Ultimately, I trust the empirical evidence that proves the compelling business case for women in leadership. This evidence proves that women are, in the very worst case, just as good at leadership as men. In my opinion they are a bit better. There is growing evidence that companies who have a larger percentage of women on their boards are out-performing those who have not. In this case, my argument supporting women in leadership becomes a rational business case and not an emotional one.

My position is this: If the board of a large company is wilfully ignoring the prevailing evidence and continuing to favour their fellow males as their preferred leadership candidates, then this amounts to gross misconduct. This is a hard-nosed strategic position that I am taking. Yes, I am frustrated and angry at the stupidity and self-serving attitudes being demonstrated, but my logical business position is that board members who commit gross misconduct are betraying their fiduciary responsibilities. They have lost shareholder trust and must be removed for the long-term good of the organisation.

Between 2004 and 2011 the number of women on the boards of the UK FTSE 100 companies grew from 9.4% to 12.5%. In 2011, the number of women on the boards of the FTSE 250 companies was 7.8%. That is pathetic. There was a 2008 quote from the Equality and Human Rights Commission which said:

"At the current rate of change it will take over 70 years to achieve gender-balanced boardrooms in the UK."

Even the higher intellect argument now favours women. The number of female graduates in the EU far exceeds their male counterparts. It was 59% in 2004 and has remained at a similar level since then. Here are some more numbers which show the difference in business performance, during the past six years, of boards with just one female executive versus boards with no female executives.

No females: Average Return on Investment (ROI) 12%

One female: Average Return on Investment (ROI) 16%

No females: Average Net Income Growth 10%

One female: Average Net Income Growth 14%

In absolute terms this is a small but significant difference, but in relative terms, the differences are 33% and 40% respectively. Another study by Catalyst in 2007 found that companies with the highest percentage of female board directors outperformed those companies with the lowest percentage by an average of 53%.

The bottom line is this: There is a positive correlation between women in leadership and business performance.

- Women on the board enhance the bottom line
- The empirical evidence is compelling
- There are not enough women on boards
- Therefore many businesses are under-performing
- Who is being held accountable?
- What if we treat people as an asset and not a cost?

- What if women are an investment and not a cost?

- What if more men support the case for women?

- Use the data to make this a strategic imperative

- Not fixing this is gross negligence.

Research from the Cranfield School of Management in 2008 suggested that not only are there fewer women in senior roles in Financial Services compared to other parts of the industry, but those women that did rise to high positions were also less likely to have children. I came across the following quote from a Swiss Insurance Company executive:

"The typical female top manager here is a single, childless foreigner."

There's a reason why I refer to The Baby Elephant in the Room. The inconvenient truth in many organisations is that because women have babies, they have expectations about work-life balance that are alien to many of their alpha male counterparts.

Within the toxic culture of the Elephant in the Room, the concept of work-life balance is a sign of weakness. In the self-serving competitive alpha male culture where it is all about the survival of the fittest, most women are disadvantaged. In fact, most sane women have the wisdom, common sense and emotional intelligence to reject such extreme conditions for leadership.

My wife is a senior manager in a large company. I was speaking at a conference in Budapest where I had included a section about women in leadership and she came along as a birthday treat. We had a very lively debate in a Budapest restaurant about the concept of maternity at work. It was so lively that we were barely on speaking terms on the way back to our hotel!

Guess who was most passionate about the maternity rights of women during the conversation. It's a complex subject and one which is very divisive, even amongst women and especially if childless women are involved in the debate. (Alison and I are childless, by the way, but I do claim the higher ground as the oldest of seven children including three girls.) She queried my position that companies should be even more radical with respect to policies supporting women who have babies, on the basis that things are difficult enough to cope with as they are. I do respect her position, which was driven by reality and pragmatism. It is such a complex, challenging debate and we were both right. I just happened to be more right!

I once had a lady working for me who was based in Germany. German law favours women on maternity leave and guarantees them a position after their return. I have no problem with this at all and wish that more countries did it. I smile when I think about how my team member planned a sequence of three pregnancies with military precision, returning for a very short time after each maternity leave period and then departing again for another lengthy period of maternity leave.

Cases like this, whether they are in Germany, the UK, or other parts of the world create a real need for companies to offer more flexible and understanding headcount policies, otherwise there is great frustration for bosses who are forced to juggle their resources in order to cope.

I read with interest some November 2013 data from a study conducted by the gender diversity campaign group Opportunity Now. Their initial findings, based on responses from 14,000 working women aged between 28 and 40, were very interesting and illuminating and pretty much reinforce everything that I have said so far.

Here are a few of them:

- 91% believe that most senior roles involve pressure, long hours and high stress levels

- 81% feel having children will affect their career progression

- 66% believe work needs to be their number one priority if they are to advance their career

- 63% feel that flexible working still means working long hours

- And just 34% believe that the opportunities to advance are equal between women who have children and those who do not.

Women who have babies are incredibly inconvenient for businesses, especially at the top, where they leave a serious talent gap while they are away from work.

Robert Baker, who I mentioned earlier, is a senior partner with the UK arm of global consulting company Mercer. Interestingly, Robert is also the one male board member of the Federation Board of the European Professional Women's Network (EPWN).

I asked Robert the following questions:

What's your Elephant in the Room?

"Many men are failing to realise the value and relevance of gender diversity to the business and to bottom line results. I think that a lot more men would get involved if they appreciated not only the powerful business case, but also the relevance for enhancing their own careers in making these connections. Gender diversity is more than just an HR initiative – it is absolutely central to a business's success. It needs to be mainstreamed from the CEO throughout the organisation."

If there was one thing that you would recommend to fellow men, what would it be?

"We need to start talking to other men who have already been proactive in this space. We also need to be bold and spread the word to the men who are not yet involved, so we create a growing community of men who not only 'get it' but who actively become advocates for gender diversity. It's not just about doing the right thing; it's about appreciating the compelling business case."

I was delighted to discover you as a fellow advocate for women in leadership through our mutual association with Catalyst. Tell me your story.

"I always enjoyed facilitating events and it was something that I was quite good at. I think I was always sensitive to women's issues and a few years ago, I facilitated an event called 'Are women's networks a waste of time?' It went well and I was invited back to facilitate another event, which also went well, leading to a request to chair a women's event in Madrid. Following this I was asked to join the steering group for Mercer's women's network and to join the Federation Board of the EPWN.

"It was fascinating for me to be the only guy working with such clever, switched on women and I have learned a lot. I continued my involvement and researched the case for women in leadership in greater depth. I linked up with John Gerzema, who wrote 'The Athena Doctrine' and saw some of the Zenger and Folkman research about women outperforming men on their characteristics of Extraordinary Leadership.

"I eventually set up some webinars for fellow male leaders to discuss how to get men more engaged in advancing women; it is clear that many of these leaders see this as a hard business case that cannot be ignored. The fact that some of our fellow male leaders do not yet get this is likely to hamper their business success, as research by organisations like Catalyst shows there's a significant outperformance by companies with greater female representation in senior leadership."

I talk about being more radical in supporting woman and I also try to get baby-related matters onto the table. Do you think we need to be more radical?

"I'm wondering if it is possible to take the baby out of the room. When women take time out to have babies, you are right that many see it as an inconvenience, but what if, for either maternity or paternity, we reflect on the sabbatical argument? People benefit from time out of the business and come back the better for the time out they have had.

"If you add the baby back into the debate, there are all the values to be gained from parenthood. You need to be incredibly organised, yet flexible, patient and people focused. The single, childless people, who may be less inconvenienced, may also be less multi-dimensional in their thinking and experience. There's a lot more to this than meets the eye."

Finally, give me some crumbs of hope. Are we winning? Are we breaking down the stereotypical thinking?

"Are we making progress? Yes. As for winning, I wonder if that ultimately equals parity. I'm encouraged by the interest and attention being shown by an increasing number of corporate leaders. Maybe we need to get the message further down the leadership organisation. The younger generation of potential leaders get it for sure."

It was great to speak to Robert Baker about our shared interest in supporting the acceleration of women into senior leadership positions. In many ways, how well we do this will be the most important determining factor of all in how well we eventually succeed in eating the Elephant in the Room.

The volume of retiring baby boomers is growing fast and as it does, the gap in the size of the pool of potential leadership talent becomes more acute. The war for talent that we have been trying to put off or simply ignore in our pursuit of short-term results becomes real at last.

Or does it?

I am wondering what happens to our battles in trying to win the war for talent if we reflect on the sheer volume of leadership talent that women provide. Have we been discounting this critical source of talent? I'm willing to bet that we have.

How to Eat the Elephant in the Room

CHAPTER TEN – Summary and Final Thoughts

I have been making a general nuisance of myself by banging on about women in leadership since I spoke at the 2006 Talent Conference in Dublin. It was always my intention that the final chapter would be on this important topic.

The evidence about the value of women in leadership is compelling. With the exception of a few companies like Mercer, most companies are wilfully ignoring the evidence. As I write these closing words, I have listened with disbelief to the idiotic words of Nigel Farage (UKIP Leader) about the lower value of women, with regards to salary, compared to men, because they have the temerity to have babies! Shareholders of companies who are wilfully ignoring the evidence need to stand up and shout:

"I'm as mad as hell and I'm not going to take this anymore!"

The evidence that stereotyping lies at the heart of the problem makes me feel that gender diversity initiatives will either fail, or not be sustainable, without the active assistance and support of an increasing number of men, like myself and Robert Baker. For my part, I will continue to speak passionately about this and spread the good news about the value of putting more women at the top.

Please feel free to share my nuggets of empirical evidence with others. Surely there is a case for you to get passionate about this as well!

How to Eat the Elephant in the Room

HOW TO EAT THE ELEPHANT IN THE ROOM

Closing Comments and Final Thoughts

When I decided to write this book, I found a company who manufactured giant cutlery and ordered a huge knife and fork, which I thought might be useful as part of my publicity work for the book. Was I unconsciously realising the magnitude of my task? The usual tools would not suffice. I needed to think and act differently.

Whilst the book is about more than just leadership, it feels like we still live in a cynical male-dominated business world and we seldom need to look very far to have that view of leadership reinforced. On behalf of customers, employees and shareholders, I say that it is time to put things right. But in order to successfully accomplish that, we must think and act differently.

Good things, if abused, will eventually be damaging.

If we fail to learn, we are learning to fail. There are clear patterns of behaviour that feed our Elephant. There is a range of things that are positive and may feel good at first, as explored in E.L.E.P.H.A.N.T. S.A.N.D.W.I.C.H, but when they are pursued to excess, things can, and frequently do, change for the worse.

We have arrived at a critical point in the UK, where leadership in the National Health Service is under close scrutiny as the result of many avoidable deaths due to poor care and poor leadership. There has been little accountability for these failings.

In Financial Services, how many leaders, apart from Fred 'The Shred' and a few others, were held accountable for their poor leadership and the frenzy of greed that led to the financial crisis of 2008? What is our attitude towards senior leaders who describe their company's clients as 'muppets'? During my brief stint in Financial Services, I frequently noticed attitudes that seemed millions of miles away from anything approaching contrition. As I write these closing words, there is already noise about the emergence of a new housing bubble in the UK. How much has truly been learned? Boom and bust has not disappeared. My own 2020 vision makes me wonder what similar issues we will be reflecting on in as little as six or seven years' time.

As I reflect on that, I'm thinking back to Chapter 7, when I talked about The Two Chasms and how I was inspired by marketing theory when I wrote it. The essence of that theory, developed by Geoffrey Moore, was that the proprietors of a business, at the 'early adopter' stage, are so focused and obsessive about hitting the big time, in this case the mainstream markets, that they fail to realise the different needs and requirements for this market and fall into a big scary chasm. In other words they fail to think and act differently and as a result, their fast early growth, for which they reward themselves handsomely, evaporates and their business quickly fails.

Exactly the same principle applies to high performing individuals, who are so obsessive and single minded about achieving the trappings of status, success and reward that being promoted to a more senior and better rewarded grade or management level provides them with. After running a lap of honour around the office, they fail to think and act differently and ultimately risk failing completely, but at great cost to the broader organisation. I think you will agree that this is not my vision of 'winning performance'.

How to Eat the Elephant in the Room

The Truck that went Round and Round the M25

To finish, I want to tell you the story about the truck that went round and round the M25 at year-end. I spent a decade at Wang throughout the 1980s and witnessed a spectacular boom and bust. It was a roller-coaster, but I truly loved working there and made many friends, including my wife, Alison.

The 1980s was an exciting time to be working in technology. We worked hard and we played even harder. I worked with some of the best salespeople around, but the focus was on 'doing the numbers'! I was frequently invited to 'steak and beans' nights, where the top performing sales people ate steak and the worst performers ate beans. It was not unusual to spend four hours at lunch with a customer, then return to the office and carry on working. It was fun. It was challenging. It was exciting!

However, during that decade I noticed that something alarming was happening. As each year progressed, a larger and larger percentage of business for the year was skewed towards the last month of a quarter and eventually, the last few days of a quarter. What was happening? It was simple. In order to 'do the numbers', especially at a time when sales bonuses were at stake, discounts were being offered. Please note that these were not discounts that were required in order to win the business from a competitor; these were discounts offered to persuade the customer to place an order, or accept a delivery, for revenue purposes, at a particular time of year.

Over time, the last few days of the year became critical for 'revenue recognition' purposes. A situation was created where savvy customers successfully created a form of 'arbitrage', where they finessed Wang's insatiable desire for revenue in order to secure unnecessary discounts by accepting delivery of equipment that

How to Eat the Elephant in the Room

they did not yet need.

Wang's external auditors allowed a short delivery window, for the purposes of revenue recognition, which went slightly beyond year-end, to allow for delivery to the customer to be completed. On occasion, it was possible to despatch a truck, full of equipment, minutes before midnight on the final day of the year and generate an invoice. We would frequently stay at work late to ensure that the invoice was generated.

In addition, it was possible that a process that we laughingly called 'driving the truck round and round the M25' might occur, whereby the delivery arrived on the customer's premises, after a suitable delay. The delivery might then be rejected by the customer, thus requiring a credit note, which was issued in the first quarter of the new financial year. The customer would then accept the new delivery when they actually required the equipment and receive a new invoice in the usual way. It was very creative, but of questionable integrity.

Sometimes, the majority of a sales person's bonus and their manager's bonus for the entire year could hinge on a single such delivery. The sales person might even win an award as a result of this trickery and perhaps be invited to attend the annual achievers trip as a result.

I struggled to come to terms with this and at year-end in 1987 I refused to sanction such a delivery. It was for a very large amount of money. After much pressure, which escalated into a massive row with the sales manager, I still refused to sanction the delivery. This put huge bonuses at risk, creating even more pressure and conflict.

Eventually, the Managing Director approved the shipment. A day or so later, I received a phone call from the warehouse and went

How to Eat the Elephant in the Room

immediately to the Finance Director's office. It was about the shipment. He asked: "What's the problem?" and I replied: "John, you won't believe this…" before collapsing into a paroxysm of laughter as I gasped, "The shipment has been stolen!" Great hilarity followed as we reviewed what had happened. The contents of the truck had been opportunistically stolen from where it had been parked overnight, awaiting completion of its trip 'round and round the M25'.

The moral of this absurd, but true, story is simple, and an appropriate one with which to end this book. Having a strong drive for results is admirable, but when it becomes all-consuming, with a single minded, self-serving focus that puts your personal needs ahead of the company and its customers, great danger lies ahead. Think twice before putting successful, extreme red, aggressive sales people in charge at the top.

And on that bombshell, my work is done.

As you put this book down and reflect on the best way for you to eat your Elephant in the Room, think about everything we have explored together. These Elephants are different. They come from different places, with different life histories and very different attitudes towards things that are important to us.

Where you take your first bite really does depend on what kind of Elephant is in the room and how deafening the unspoken truth is. But know this: once you make a start, you can and will get there, one bite at a time!

How to Eat the Elephant in the Room